DOING
GOOD
better!

"Doing Good Better! is the best there is."

"A crisply written and highly practical book offering consistently sound commonsense advice on the real-life problems and challenges of nonprofit board service. Doing Good Better *could serve as well for independent directors of a Fortune 500 company as it does for the board of any of our nation's more than one million nonprofits."*

—**Richard F. Celeste**, Governor of Ohio (1983-1991)

"A very fine book on board leadership of nonprofit organizations. This particular book will be very beneficial to many people who are members of nonprofit boards across the country."

—**Millard Fuller**, president and founder,
Habitat for Humanity, International

"A very readable book and full of wisdom. A commonsense approach based on the depth of much experience."

—**Sherburne Laughlin**,
Executive Director, Support Center of Washington

DOING GOOD

GOOD

better!

How to be an Effective
Board Member
of a Nonprofit Organization

EDGAR STOESZ and CHESTER RABER

Good Books

Intercourse, PA 17534

ACKNOWLEDGEMENTS
We gratefully recognize the work of Phyllis Horst Nafziger for her
care in typing this manuscript (several times)
and the efforts of Phyllis Pellman Good for her editing,
which increased the book's readability.

Design by Dawn J. Ranck
Cover design and illustrations by Cheryl Benner

DOING GOOD BETTER
Copyright © 1994 by Good Books
Intercourse, Pennsylvania 17534
International Standard Book Number: 1-56148-099-1
Library of Congress Catalog Card Number: 94-7314

Library of Congress Cataloging-in-Publication Data

Stoesz, Edgar.
    Doing good better! : how to be an effective board member of a nonprofit
organization / Edgar Stoesz and Chester Raber.
        p. cm.
    Includes bibliographical references.
    ISBN 1-56148-099-1 : $9.95
    1. Nonprofit organizations--Management. 2. Directors of corporations.
I. Raber, Chester. II. Title.
HD62.6.S76   1994
658'.048--dc20   94-7314
                                                                        CIP

This book is dedicated to
Gladys Stoesz
and
Gerry Raber.

TABLE OF CONTENTS

INTRODUCTION

Nonprofit organizations are about doing good. This book is about helping them to do it *better*. Its purpose is to raise the level of board service so that organizations will more nearly perform their potential.

This book is directed to the men and women who believe, like we do, in helping others through the medium of a nonprofit organization. We intend it to be a practical book which speaks to real life situations. We draw heavily from what we have experienced and observed, although we are also informed by what others have written on the subject. We do not put forward a new science of organizations. We offer a commonsense approach to the subject, grounded in sound theory with a dash of idealism.

We have deliberately narrowed our focus to nonprofits to make the subject more manageable, although most of what we say applies to any organization. Even within this narrowed definition we deal with both the religious and the secular, well established groups as well as those which are not yet legally incorporated, organizations as disparate as schools, camps, Alcoholics Anonymous, Mothers Against Drunk Driving, and mutual insurance companies. With all their diversity, nonprofits share one thing in common—the desire to fulfill their missions more effectively and faithfully. That, too, is our intention.

This is not pleasure reading. What matters is that, as a result of reading this book, you will be able to lead more effectively and better prepare your organization to face the future.

—Edgar Stoesz and Chester Raber

1.

___

ORGANIZATIONS:
Why Are They Needed?

> *"People are setting themselves more and more goals that can be accomplished only through large expenditures of money and large scale organizational efforts. . . . Such goals can be achieved only by harnessing vast resources of talent, money and organizational strength. That is one of the reasons we have moved, as every modern society must, towards larger and more complex patterns of organization."*
> —John W. Gardner

Most public services are supplied either by business or the government. There are, however, gaps and deficiencies, including a wide variety of human needs which fall between the cracks. Among these are housing, education, health, human services, religion, art, and culture. Privately supported, self-governing nonprofit organizations fulfill urgent personal and community needs which are a crucial part of a healthy civilization.

Stages Of An Organization

Nonprofit organizations generally enjoy a good reputation. The record is not, however, without blemish.

The Philadelphia Inquirer, in the spring of 1993, ran a seven-part investigative series which concluded that the nations' "non-profit economy has become a huge virtually unregulated industry." It disclosed such abuses as high salaries, high fund-raising costs and lean accomplishments. In truth, most nonprofits under-perform their potential. This is the challenge which faces directors of nonprofit organizations.

The size and importance of the nonprofit sector is not generally known or acknowledged. There are, according to United States Government estimates, 1,140,000 nonprofit organizations in the United States. Approximately 400,000 are member-serving, that is, professional associations and chambers of commerce, while 740,000 are public-serving, working, for example, in culture and aiding the poor.

In 1990, Americans contributed $123 billion to various charitable causes. About 90% of that amount came from individuals and the remaining 10% from corporations and foundations. More than half was given to religious organizations. The U.S. tax law contains 26 separate sections under which public service nonprofits can claim exemption from federal income tax.

Not only are there many different kinds of organizations, but organizations go through stages of development and, accordingly, have differing characteristics and needs. (See Figure 1.)

Founders are the driving forces who call organizations into existence. They see clearly focused service opportunities which need to be addressed. In the earliest stage, the founder is prominent. But, to be an effective organization, the circle must eventually expand to include others.

This was certainly true of Habitat for Humanity International. It grew out of the conviction of Clarence

FIGURE 1

Stages of an Organization

I. In the beginning there is a founder.

X

II. There are converts.

xx**X**xx

III. A Board is organized, complete with Board Committees (BC). Volunteers (V) come forward to help.

xxx**X**xxx
BC VVVVV BC

IV. More Board Committees are organized, more volunteers come forward, and now there are also a few employees (e).

xxxx**X**xxxx
BC VVVVVVV eeeee BC
BC VVVVVVV   BC
VVVVVVV
VVVVVVV

V. A CEO is employed and charged with the responsibility of carrying out the mission in accordance with the policies prescribed by the board.

xxxx**X**xxxx
BC   CEO   BC
BC   BC
VVVVVVV eeeee
VVVVVVV eeeee
VVVVVVV
VVVVVVV

Some organizations advance from Stage I to Stage V and beyond in a few years. Some get stalled. Some die. The needs of an organization and the role of a Board change according to the organization's stage of development.

Jordan—a theologian/farmer—and Millard Fuller—a lawyer/entrepreneur—that shacks are an abomination to God and an offense to a community. Their vision was quickly joined by other people of goodwill and resulted in a movement which encircled the globe and which, even 18 years later, is still picking up momentum.

Founders are activists. They are risk-takers. They are driven by a vision. They get an idea and enlist the participation of others. These qualities need to be adapted as the organization matures, but special recognition belongs to the brave and visionary souls who pioneer organizations.

Eventually—sooner for some than for others—it becomes clear that the needs of an organization have changed. The founders can no longer do it all. There is too much work, and some tasks need specialized attention. The vision exceeds what the founders are able to accomplish.

This is the stage at which an organization either stalls, or a new vision or energies come forward. Frequently, employed staff join the volunteers. With this step usually come more formal policies and a steady stream of income. As the initiative shifts from the volunteer founders to the salaried employees, the former may lose control. The founder and charter members generally fear that the vision is being compromised. Yet the work grows in spite of uncertainty and threat.

Typically an organization reaches a crisis point which requires further major adjustments. As the work has grown, the staff has gotten larger. The founding board is replaced by directors who, even though they share the vision, express it differently. Original board members who continue may feel they are losing control. They may be tempted to accuse the staff of not keeping the board sufficiently informed. And when board members request information or make suggestions, they may be charged with meddling or engaging in "micro-management."

Staff may feel that the board, instead of leading the organization, is a heavy weight to endure. Communication between them becomes minimal and misdirected. Frustration abounds. Joy disappears. Crisis threatens.

While the names and places vary, these are the passages many organizations experience. Some die in the process. Others reach a plateau and grasp for life. Some find their way through a series of ups and downs and survive in robust health.

The point is that organizational needs change over time. In the beginning creativity and spontaneity abound. Increased size, however, brings with it the need for more accountability, leading to increased institutionalization, which is traditionally resisted by founders. We believe institutionalization is the inevitable result of growth and a sign of maturity. The choice of a rapidly growing organization is not *whether* it will institutionalize, but whether it will become a *good* institution or a bad one.

Good institutions can be recognized by how consistently and effectively they perform their mission and by how effectively they renew themselves. The organization which refuses to grow up will remain in an adolescent state, limiting its effectiveness.

Even the board of an organization that has evolved to Stage V must discover new ways to accomplish its mission. Instead of planning a day at a time, a Stage V organization must identify a clear vision and put appropriate long-term plans in place. It needs to delegate responsibility to carefully selected individuals who are given clear job descriptions and key performance indicators. Its board must stay in good communication with the stakeholders to whom it is accountable and with the staff which is accountable to it. Stakeholders are those who have a stake in the organization, including employees and clients. They may also be contributors who expect the organization to perform certain services to which they are committed.

Organizational Changes That Are Likely to Come

Effective directors continually read the environment and create change. They understand that the future is not just a continuation of the past. Though many fundamentals will remain, we believe that the following trends in society will change the way nonprofit organizations do their work.

1. There will be increased demand for more active roles for women.

2. More exacting legal responsibilities will emerge.

3. Many persons will have more leisure time and less cash, compared to the past.

4. More effort will need to be expended to win and keep the public trust.

5. There will be pronounced intolerance of sloth and amateurism.

6. Globalization and multiculturalism will increase.

Organizations, like the people who run them, have their limitations, but a society can be judged by the effectiveness of the organizations it maintains. Organizations permit us to do collectively what no one can do alone. Persons who serve in religious organizations may even see their work as a part of God's ongoing work of creation.

2.

TRUSTEES:
Their Roles and Responsibilities

> *"There is one thing all boards have in common—they do not function."*
> — Peter F. Drucker

Organizations are "owned" by all who have a stake in them. They do not just exist in a detached state. Every one of those 1,140,000 nonprofit organizations in the United States are owned by someone for some defined purpose. The rights and responsibilities of ownership are delegated to a Board of Directors. Directors, it is important to recognize, do not own the organization; instead, they are trustees who act on behalf of those who do. They have both a moral and a legal responsibility to act in a prudent and trustworthy manner.

What Should a Board **Not** Do?

What sorts of board behavior might lead to the allegation with which this chapter begins? What habits should boards and board members unlearn?

- Failing to lead.
- Getting lost in details and concentrating on minutia.
- Meddling at the operational level.

- Failing to focus adequately on the future.
- Delegating without giving clear expectations and guiding policies.
- Being reactionary and not sufficiently proactive.
- Managing instead of leading.
- Confusing action with effectiveness.
- Being too self-satisfied.
- Being too busy.

The Responsibilities of the Board

The major responsibilities of a board can be divided into three categories: 1) to identify the vision and the mission; 2) to delegate the implementation of the mission; 3) to ensure the availability of necessary resources.

Vision/Mission

The first duty of the Board is to provide a convincing answer to the questions, Why should this organization exist? What is our vision for its mission? What are the expectations of the stakeholders?

Most organizations begin with a vision of something which needs to be done. Vision must be focused and bold.

The three "musts" for successful mission, according to Peter F. Drucker, are:

1. **Need:** For a nonprofit, need is opportunity, and the more compelling and urgent the need, the greater the opportunity.

2. **Competence:** Nonprofits should focus on what they already know something about. Experts outside of their field of competence are amateurs.

3. **Commitment:** An activity should be selected because the directors think that it is the most important thing they could be doing. Directors should endorse an organization only if they are committed to it.

A mission statement should be short and focused.

Habitat for Humanity says clearly that its goal is "to eliminate poverty housing from the face of the earth by year 2000." The Girl Scouts of America state simply, "To help each girl reach her own highest potential." A mission statement should be operational; otherwise it is just good intentions. Whereas goal-setting is done annually, a mission statement is "forever."

Delegation, Guided by Policies

The second duty of a board is to provide for the implementation of the vision. The profound words of a mission statement need to find their way into action if the organization is to have any integrity (and future). Boards do very little of the *doing* themselves. They discharge their duties through delegation.

Delegation is more than saying to someone, "Do as you think best." Early in my (Edgar) career I was asked by a boss, whom I admired greatly, to visit a major Mennonite aid program in Newfoundland. I was taken aback. Why me? What was I expected to accomplish? The telegraphic answer was, "We need to see what your eyes will see and hear what your ears will hear." While long on affirmation, it was lacking in content!

Delegation needs to be guided by well formulated written policies which are built on experience and which state the values and the perceptions the board wants to preserve. Through its policies, a board exercises proactive leadership. Policies are, we are convinced, a powerful and under-recognized governance tool.

A good exercise for every board is to occasionally assemble and review all policies it has adopted. This can be a humbling experience. While seeing themselves as a policy-making body, many boards are embarrassed to discover that they haven't adopted as many operational policies as they had thought, and several that do exist are no longer relevant. Some are not being enforced and others appear downright embarrassing.

I (Chet) worked with an organization whose leaders were frustrated and discouraged. The board was dissatisfied with how things were being done. One day they realized that, while they had delegated responsibility to the administration, they had not given adequate guidance through accompanying policy statements. Once this omission was corrected, performance and morale increased noticeably.

On the other hand, a board cannot and should not attempt to adopt a policy statement for every imaginable contingency. Just as an organization can be guilty of not providing sufficient guidance, so it can go to the other extreme and become policy-bound.

John Carver, in his excellent book, *Boards That Make a Difference*, suggests that some policy-making is done best by stating what will *not* be tolerated. This may appear negative, but to clarify the boundaries of acceptable action, and to state what is unacceptable, can prove to be a freeing experience.

Carver is of the opinion that the establishment of limitations is especially relevant to executives. In an attempt to act responsibly, boards sometimes impose limitations which interfere and demoralize. Executives need to be empowered, they need to be set free, but within a broadly defined structure which can, according to Carver, be expressed in fewer than 10 basic Executive Limitation policies.

Clear and appropriate delegation also includes establishing key performance indicators. Organizations need to keep score. Are we doing what we said we would? Are we getting good value for the contributed dollar? The board of a private school should be watching how its students are testing and what its student retention is.

Always directors must be asking themselves, is our mission being accomplished?

Nonprofit institutions, according to Drucker, tend not to give priority to performance and results. Many report inputs in great detail but give scant review to outputs. Evaluation is concerned with outputs. Directors need to monitor whether the identified mission is being accomplished. Employees have a right to know by what criteria their performance will be measured.

Nonprofit directors must continually strive toward excellence. Sloth cannot be tolerated. Commitment to quality cannot be satisfied by sending employees to a seminar or by posting reminders on the bulletin board. It must be part of the management philosophy.

Resources

An organization may have an inspiring mission statement. It may have an excellent strategy for the implementation of its plan. The crucial question which remains is, Does it have the necessary resources?

Organizations need to maintain a balance between vision and reality. Performance dare not lag far behind pronouncements. Vision has its place, but organizations also need to do periodic reality checks.

Personnel and money are among an organization's most valuable resources. It is almost axiomatic, and yet often ignored, that organizations are only as effective as the people who staff them. What is unique about nonprofits is the mixing of volunteers and paid staff. Volunteers are the heart of many nonprofits. By their dedication and contribution of time they make possible what would otherwise be unaffordable. Given today's shortened workweek and earlier retirement practices, along with longer life expectancy and less expendable cash, nonprofits do well to maximize this valuable resource.

Achieving a specific objective with volunteers who come and go is a special management challenge. Volunteers need to be wisely supervised for maximum effectiveness. They have a right to expect that something worthwhile will result from their effort. Our experience is that volunteers are best utilized alongside experienced staff who help to provide the needed oversight and continuity.

The employment records of nonprofits leave much to be desired. The persistent drive to get the maximum bang for the buck and the tendency to trade on the goodwill of dedicated employees result in unfortunate experiences. By way of comparison, it has been helpful for me (Edgar), a longtime nonprofit manager, to observe how well my son is treated by his Fortune 500 employer.

The second major resource, money, is dealt with in Chapter 8 and is therefore not discussed in detail here. Suffice it to say that directors are responsible to ensure that the resources needed to fill the identified mission are available.

Organizations which perform effectively in these three categories—vision/mission, delegation, and resources—are probably doing well. Organizations who are experiencing difficulties can probably trace their causes to a deficiency in one of these three areas.

Conflict of Interest

The term itself is interesting. It recognizes that directors have more than one interest in board service. They sincerely want to help. At the same time, they also want and deserve personal satisfaction from the experience. Many who serve on boards are prompted by both altruistic and personal motives.

When do these interests conflict? Trouble comes when personal and organizational activities intersect. When there is a dual interest or the appearance of a dual interest, directors must take steps to preserve or enhance the public trust. The organizational interest must always take precedence over all other business and personal interests.

For example, directors could be in conflict of interest if they offer to sell real estate to the organization on whose board they serve, even if the selling price is at or below the appraised or market value. Similarly, if a board member contemplates purchasing or leasing property that the organization may wish to purchase, the board member may be placed in a conflict of interest situation.

When directors are confronted with an actual or apparent conflict of interest, it is important for them to preserve the organization's integrity by taking reasonable steps to disclose this information to others on the board. A director may have to resign if the transaction is major or substantial. Minimally, the director must inform the board of the important facts and details and must abstain from voting on the transaction. These actions should be recorded in the minutes to document the disclosure.

The same principles apply to smaller transactions. Each board should discuss the duty of loyalty and conflicts of interest on a regular basis. Not only is the public sensitive to self-dealing, but such activities can be the basis for a suit against the directors and officers (see Chapter 13, Legal Dimensions).

For a checklist of board functions, see Exhibit 8, Annual Board Self-Assessment.

Board Membership

Where are the valuable people to be found who will serve in this important capacity?

Organizations are rightfully judged by the people associated with them. Directors who are respected in the wider community automatically confer respect on the organization they represent. This is illustrated by the inestimable value that Jimmy and Rosalynn Carter bring to Habitat for Humanity. It is instructive to point out, however, that the Carter support is so valuable because it is authentic. They don't just show up for photo opportunities. They contribute their sweat equity along with the rest.

A board is only as capable as the combined talents and experience of its individual members, plus the synergism which results from their interaction. No given director possesses all desirable qualities in full measure. This is precisely the role of an institution. What one person lacks is supplemented by the gifts of another. Through positive interaction the directors stimulate each other, so that in an effective institution the whole is greater than the sum of its parts (members). (Sadly, the opposite is also true; a board dynamic can be negative.)

In the search for effective directors, consideration should be given to the following traits.

1. **Compatibility.** Do the prospective candidates live the values and lifestyle your organization advocates? Have they proven themselves to be persons of compassion and generous spirit? Are they already supporters of your organization or similar causes? Have they been or are they currently associated with activities which will reflect negatively on your organization? Be wary of excessive self-interest and negative associations.

2. **Enthusiasm.** People cannot excite others without first being excited themselves. Ralph Waldo Emerson said it succinctly. "Nothing was ever accomplished without enthusiasm."

3. **Judgment.** Judgment results from combining wisdom with experience. We have known directors who are knowledgeable and dedicated but who lacked the rare ability to sort through complex issues and arrive at a sound conclusion. A director who invariably agrees with

the last person who spoke, or who always votes with the majority, is of little value. Good directors are capable of independent judgment, while at the same time allowing their insights to be enriched by interaction with their fellow directors.

4. **Just.** A valuable board member is persistent in the pursuit of right. Brian O'Connell in his helpful book, *The Board Member Book*, calls it the single most important quality a director can possess.

Knowing what is right can be very difficult, but a board is more likely to *do* what is right if it makes that its conscious objective. Boards are prone to compromise, to look for the easy out. Members are quick to ask, What if. . . ? They are pre-disposed to contain a controversy and may lose sight of the basic question, What is right? A board who fears the imagined consequences of acting on what it believes to be right can anticipate worse consequences.

5. **Teamwork.** The work of a board is, by definition, a collective process. It is also a delicate process which can be upset by even one individual who demands too much air time or who acts in an inflexible, arrogant manner. Lone rangers aren't good directors.

6. **What about specialized expertise?** Is the ideal board one where the most successful corporate executive is the chair, the newspaper editor is the secretary, the banker is the treasurer, and the pastor serves as chaplain, while the lawyer serves as parliamentarian? Not necessarily.

A well-rounded board should include people of divergent backgrounds. They will naturally have specializations, but board members should not see themselves as representing particular interests. All board members should regard themselves as part of a group representing the whole membership.

7. **What about inside directors?** There is no consensus about whether employees should be permitted

to serve on the board. This practice is more common in the for-profit than the nonprofit sector. One advantage is that staff have firsthand knowledge of the operation's realities. The practice also has some obvious dangers. One of them, ironically, is that it has a tendency to focus the board discussion too much at the operational level. We feel that having staff as board members should be done selectively, if at all, and never below the CEO level. Management can always be invited to participate in a discussion when the board believes that its contribution would be useful.

Once a board has selected the persons it wants to include in its membership, how does it proceed to invite them? One of the most common mistakes is to define the demands of directorship downward, fearing that the person will decline the invitation because s/he is too busy. Not only does that risk giving false information, more importantly it can destroy the urgency and the challenge of the invitation. Board recruiters should remember that only small fish bite on small bait. Strong people are looking for challenges which deserve their support.

Persons respond to an invitation to board service based partly on who extends the invitation, when, and how. The invitation should be extended by someone who is able to convey its importance. Persons should not be asked at the height of their busy seasons. When the right persons are asked in the right way, the chances of them responding favorably are significantly increased. Sometimes it is most effective to invite persons to serve years in advance of their actual starting date.

Sustained Effectiveness

Many boards achieve spurts of genius, followed by embarrassing relapses. Some boards do not make the transition to the next stage as discussed in Chapter 1.

Other boards get bogged down in mediocrity or conflict. Many get distracted, disenchanted, and bored. How can a board achieve sustained effectiveness?

The responsibility for board effectiveness is assigned to the chairperson. Many boards are not clear on this point. It is, we feel, improper to assign this function to the CEO or to permit him/her to act in this capacity. The board does not work for the CEO. The CEO works for the board and should not control it.

For sustained effectiveness there needs to be some turnover in board membership. Dead wood should not be permitted. Board membership needs to change to reflect changing circumstances. Just as in plant life, where the bloom comes from the new growth, so new directors bring new life to an organization. They ask questions old directors are no longer asking. They attempt, and sometimes achieve, what old directors *know* is not possible.

Every board should, we believe, establish a maximum term of service that is between six and nine years. The problems that such a limitation brings are, in our experience, preferred to the problems and bad feelings which result when directors are allowed to assume election is for life. Term limits deliver the message that directors have limited time to make their contributions. The feelings of directors who have rendered many years of faithful service should not be disregarded, but neither should organizational effectiveness be sacrificed. (This subject is discussed in more detail in Chapter 15, Leaving Right.)

Another way to achieve sustained effectiveness is by undergoing internal evaluation. Some boards have a special board development committee which is elected by the board (not appointed by the chair) to perform this function, along with the nominating process. Some board directors evaluate each other. Some do this annually, while others do it only when a member is being considered for another term of service. Minimally, board members should evaluate their own performance and set goals for themselves annually.

Our final suggestion is that board effectiveness can be enhanced through director education. Having recruited the best directors available, effective boards then proceed to help their members grow and become even more effective. This process begins with a good orientation program (see Exhibit 2, Orientation of Board Members). It is furthered through board retreats and on-the-job training. Effective boards plan for the growth of their directors (and employees) and, in turn, benefit from their increased performance.

Board service is a rare honor. It is a humbling responsibility. It is, if we are going to do it conscientiously, hard work. To speak about "sitting on a board" is an unfortunate misnomer. We view board service as an opportunity to contribute ourselves to a cause in which we believe. Through service on boards that make a difference, we are able to improve our surroundings and better the lives of our fellow humans and, in the process, find our own lives enriched.

3.

GOVERNANCE:
Distributing the Task

> *"'It is not right!' his father-in-law exclaimed. 'You're going to wear yourself out—and if you do, what will happen to the people? Moses, this burden is too heavy for you to handle all by yourself.*
>
> *"'Now listen and let me give you a word of advice, and let God bless you. . . . Find some capable, godly, honest men who hate bribes and appoint them as judges, one judge for each 1000 people; he in turn will have ten judges under him, each in charge of a hundred; and under each of them will be two judges, each responsible for the affairs of fifty people, and each of these will have five judges beneath him, each counseling ten people. If you follow this advice, and if the Lord agrees, you will be able to endure the pressure, and there will be peace and harmony in the camp.'"*
>
> —Exodus 18:17-23

One of a board's most basic responsibilities is to define itself. In the beginning (Stages I and II of an organization's life), the board does it all. But as an organization grows and matures, its task exceeds what a board can expect from its members. At this point a board must decide what it will do and what it will delegate. A board must do this defining itself. No one else can do it for them. This decision will greatly affect the health and activity of the organization.

A board quickly develops a pattern of how it works. Some of these habits are good, while others interfere with the organization achieving its ultimate potential. How should a board work on the agenda it has chosen for itself?

Ends And Means

Organizational leaders ought to make a conscious distinction between *Ends* and *Means*. Ends are intended outcomes. They are the mission an organization has identified for itself. Means are the procedures by which the Ends are accomplished. Program activities are, by this definition, Means.

The Ends identify *what* should be done. The Means clarify *how*. Neither should be thought of as more important than the other. Both are necessary. The German proverb says it well: "One hand washes the other."

A helpful, though somewhat oversimplified, definition is that the board is responsible to identify Ends while the administration is responsible for the Means. In fact, the administration should participate in identifying the Ends. Furthermore, the board is responsible to establish the policies which will control the Means by which the Ends are achieved. The board is also responsible to keep the whole process under review. The distinction, while not absolute, is nevertheless helpful.

An End a board may identify is to construct ten houses or to add a new unit or to raise a million dollars. In so doing, the board needs to satisfy itself that the Means will be available, but the task of devising a plan for how this is accomplished typically is assigned to the administration.

A common failing of boards is that they concentrate their efforts on Means issues. There are reasons for this tendency. First, most directors are, in their everyday lives, more actively involved in Means-type activity. Means are actions, and that is what most boards enjoy.

Second, most issues are presented to the board in Means form: How should _____ be done? Issues need to be reformulated into the Ends form: What is the desired outcome?

Third, Ends are by comparison less tangible; they must be addressed strategically. They must fit into the whole. Boards need to continually call themselves to focus on the desired Ends.

When the Habitat board decided to concentrate on Ends issues, it had the immediate effect of shortening the board's agenda and sharpening its focus. The board and, even more, the committees of the board, came to see that they had been excessively involved with Means issues. It was apparent at the same time that the board was not adequately defining the desired Ends. The board had, in fact, fallen into the trap many boards find themselves in—that of doing the work of the administration while abdicating its leadership, Ends-defining role.

In a small organization, the board both makes and implements policy. There is no administration. Many boards work this way happily and effectively. Problems arise when the needs of an organization exceed what the members are able to contribute. In such situations the tendency is for members to get so busy *doing* that the development of the organization is neglected. An organization whose members spend most of their time in the trenches instead of the boardroom may be stunted in its development. The directors are working hard but not at the right things. Their organization is in Stage III while the demands placed on them, or the goals they have set for themselves, call for them to be a Stage V organization (see page 7). The task of a board is to design a system of governance so that the function of the organization is carried out *and* the needs of the whole organization are provided for.

Boards which reserve too much of the action (Means) to themselves predictably find themselves overworked. On the other extreme, boards that define themselves too narrowly deal themselves out of the action. They are not

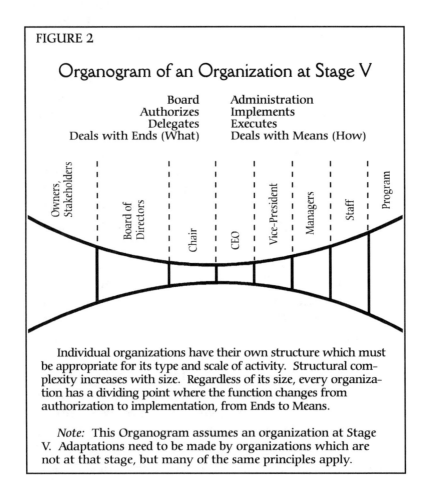

FIGURE 2

Organogram of an Organization at Stage V

Board	Administration
Authorizes	Implements
Delegates	Executes
Deals with Ends (What)	Deals with Means (How)

Owners, Stakeholders — Board of Directors — Chair — CEO — Vice-President — Managers — Staff — Program

Individual organizations have their own structure which must be appropriate for its type and scale of activity. Structural complexity increases with size. Regardless of its size, every organization has a dividing point where the function changes from authorization to implementation, from Ends to Means.

Note: This Organogram assumes an organization at Stage V. Adaptations need to be made by organizations which are not at that stage, but many of the same principles apply.

relevant to what is going on and earn the accusation of being a figurehead body. Every Board must identify a responsible role for itself and must be alert to changing as the organization grows and matures.

Use of Board Committees

Once a board has defined what functions it reserves to itself, it must make the next important distinction—what it will do as a whole group and to what extent it will use board committees. John Carver suggests that, to begin, a board should do the whole job itself and should appoint committees only as necessary.

Some boards use committees extensively while others hardly use them at all. The Habitat board, for example, maintains six standing committees and requires that each director serve on two of them. Most issues come to the board through a committee. More time is spent in committee meetings than in meetings of the whole board.

Boards use committees for a combination of reasons. The main ones are limited meeting time and full agendas. Distributing tasks to board committees permits more attention to be given to larger issues. It permits directors to concentrate on their field of competence without making spectators out of the rest of the board.

For all their value, committees of the board also have their downside. Four common problems, if acknowledged and understood, should not dissuade boards from using committees, but should help them use them more effectively.

1. **Fragmentation.** Subdividing a board into functional categories (finance, personnel, etc.) permits a board to do more in-depth work. At the same time, this can fragment a board which must, in reality, function only as an integrated system. Ask the director of a committee-dominated board about a specific action and

the common reply is, "I don't know. That is handled in another committee."

I, (Edgar), am serving on the program committee of a board. We draw up ambitious and creative plans, only to have the finance committee tell us, "Sorry, the funds aren't there." Then we need to go back and scale down our plans. Not only have we lost motion in this process, we have more than a little frustration.

2. **Dual authority.** Board committees can distract from the administrative process, creating a sort of two-headed monster. More than one executive has found him-/herself caught in the middle of this misunderstanding. A board cannot, on the one hand, hold an executive responsible for results and, on the other hand, authorize a parallel authority. Board committees should not do work that is within the parameters of an executive's legitimate function.

3. **Superficiality and redundancy.** If a board gives its automatic approval to the proposals of a committee with the customary flair of thanks and commendation, but without seriously probing the issues, it is acting superficially. Committees like this response, and action of this sort helps to speed up meetings, but is the board making wise decisions? If, on the other hand, a board insists on an in-depth reexamination of a committee's recommendations, it is being redundant. Committee morale goes down and meetings get long. The proper balance must be found.

4. **Unintended and unforeseen consequences.** Like the fabled British knight, board committees mount their steeds with enthusiasm and madly ride off in all directions. An action may make sense from the perspective of a given committee, but it may have unintended and unforeseen consequences for other parts of the organization. The unfortunate result is that such an

28

action must be reconsidered, and that is lost motion.

The program committee of an organization with which we are familiar recommended the initiation of a new service. They viewed it as a bold and creative action which was long overdue. When the recommendation was presented to the board, the immediate response from the personnel committee was, "And how do you plan to staff it? We have unfilled positions now." To which the finance committee added, "And how will it be financed? We are recommending a five percent reduction in the expenditure budget." The board process must synthesize the interests and capabilities of the whole organization.

A special word of warning about executive committees. Executive committees are, by definition, composed of the most influential directors. When they bring a recommendation, the rest of the board is hard pressed to do other than approve it. This can, unless restraint is exercised, render board members who do not serve on the executive committee powerless and demoralized.

Boards need to define both the assignment and the authority of committees it appoints. The only decision-making authority a committee has is what has been delegated to it by the board, which retains the ultimate responsibility. The best use of board committees, in our opinion, is to prepare carefully selected Ends issues for board action. Board committees should do pre-board work, not sub-board work (See Exhibit 5, General Outline for Board Committee Accountability).

Before a board concludes hastily that it can solve the problem of an overloaded agenda by delegating more functions to committees, it should analyze its agenda. Is the board spending too much time on Means issues? Are they using meeting time wisely by adhering to the doctrine of completed staff (and committee) work? (See Chapter

7.) Many nonprofit boards use more board and committee meeting time than do big corporations such as General Motors.

Delegation to the Administration

Once a board has decided what functions it will perform itself, either as a committee of the whole or through the use of board committees, its next responsibility is to delegate program administration to the staff, which is under the direction of a Chief Executive Officer. The term Chief Executive Officer (CEO) comes from the corporate world and refers to the person who directs the operational affairs of an organization. It has also come to have wide usage in nonprofit organizations, replacing such titles as Administrator or Executive Director. He/she is the only employee directly accountable to the board. All other employees are accountable to him/her. The CEO should have broad but defined authority. A CEO is responsible for results, for the implementation of the mission within policies prescribed by the board. The board should additionally spell out its expectations of the CEO by providing written key performance indicators, which can then become the basis for the CEO's annual performance review.

John Carver suggests that a board should also state explicitly what it will not tolerate in a policy statement known as Executive Limitations. He mentions specifically imprudent and unethical practices, which can be spelled out in a policy statement of ten or fewer points. A CEO, for example, who seriously overspends income or carries inadequate insurance on its vehicles, is behaving imprudently. A CEO who violates federal or state regulations is obviously being unethical.

Having stated both what it expects of a CEO and what it will not tolerate, a board is free to concentrate on other parts of its assignment. The board has appropriately addressed Ends issues, thus freeing the CEO to work at Means within a well defined framework.

The CEO has a right to expect the support of the board. When differences arise, they should be dealt with by the board. Remember that a board functions as a board only when it is in session. Board members should never put the CEO or members of the staff in a position of doing official board business when the board is not in session. Individual directors may request information from the administration, but even this is best done in the board meeting, or certainly with the knowledge of the chair. Nor should the CEO seek out the support of individual board members, especially when tension exists between the CEO and board.

If a serious dispute arises between the CEO and the board which cannot be resolved to the satisfaction of both, the CEO must be replaced. Leaving an unsupported CEO in office is not an option. As long as a CEO is in office, a board is obligated to support him/her. For more information on CEO evaluation, see Exhibit 5, Board Appraisal of the Chief Executive Officer.

Delegation by the CEO

The board delegates to the CEO, who in turn delegates to the employees who report to him/her. (This also applies to board members, when and if they serve in a staff capacity, a practice we do not recommend.) Most organizations grant the CEO the authority to hire staff for approved positions and to fire staff. (Before new positions are defined, they must be approved by the board.) Every employee should have a job description which clarifies how and when evaluations take place. Evaluation summaries should be kept in an employee's permanent file.

CEOs should describe their organization visually in the form of an organizational chart. Organizational charts should be updated annually and a copy should be supplied to the board for information purposes. It is an important document, but it is clearly concerned with Means (and not Ends), and thus it belongs first to the CEO and only secondarily to the board.

We subscribe to what is referred to as a two-tiered span of supervision. By this we mean that the board appoints a CEO, and, upon her/his recommendation, the board also approves all administrative staff directly responsible to the CEO. The CEO in turn appoints all administrative staff immediately responsible to her/him, and, upon these administrators' recommendations, the CEO approves all staff directly responsible to them. This two-tiered system applies throughout the entire organization in the fashion illustrated below.

This procedure applies also to supervision and evaluation. It limits how deep any supervisory person can reach into the organization. A board who is not satisfied with the performance of a vice president, for example, must act through the CEO to whom the vice president reports.

Board dealings with staff must all go through the CEO, whom it appoints. Board members must be careful not to meddle and not to engage in micro-management. This requires discipline, since directors are by nature drawn to

FIGURE 3

	Board	CEO	VPs	Director	Supervisor
CEO	appoints				
VPS	approves	appoints			
Director		approves	appoints		
Supervisor			approves	appoints	
Foreman				approves	appoints
Clerk					approves

act on problems which come to their attention.

Organizations are deceptively complex. This is due in part to the fact that they are made up of humans whose conduct is subject to moods and changing circumstances. An effective organization moderates these tendencies and makes processes more rational.

Board service is complicated by the fact that directors play different roles in different organizations. In one board I may serve as chair, in another President and CEO, in still another I may be a newly elected director and hold no office. Each of these organizations do business in a different way. My role in each of them is different. Always my conduct must be appropriate (and effective) in that setting.

A well functioning organization passes this test: everyone—from the board to the CEO to the entry level clerical person—understands his/her role, feels secure in it, and functions to his/her highest potential. An organization functions at its potential only to the extent that this happens consistently.

A tempering word: John W. Gardner wisely states in his book, *No Easy Victories,* "Put your faith in ideas, ideals, movements, goals. Don't put your faith in organizations. Human beings are forever building the church and killing the creed. They give such loving attention to organizational forms that the spirit is imprisoned."

Max DePree, the highly successful chairman of the Herman Miller Company and author of *The Art of Leadership,* says simply, "Relationships count more than Structure."

Peter M. Senge offers a helpful discussion of the need to view organizations as an integrated system in his excellent book, *The Fifth Discipline.* Senge writes that "vision without systems thinking ends up painting lovely pictures of the future with no understanding of the forces which must be mastered to move from here to there."

4.

LEADERSHIP:
Showing the Way

> *"The mark of a leader, the attribute that puts him in a position to show the way for others, is that he is better than most to point the way."*
> —Robert Greenleaf, *The Servant Leader*
>
> *"If anyone would be first, he must be last and servant of all."*
> —Jesus

Leaders Lead

An organization is a living organism which is constantly in a state of becoming. It is reaching out into the unknown to do what its supporters believe needs to be done. In a state of leaderlessness, it drifts and falls apart. To be effective, to survive in a competitive and rapidly changing world, organizations need to be led.

Effective leaders—not just nominal ones—cause people to want to follow. They do this by example, by the force of their personalities, and by selecting causes so compelling that people willingly sacrifice themselves for them.

Leadership should come from everywhere within a dynamic organization; it does not center only around the designated leader. Good leaders stimulate others to lead. DePree says, "The art of leadership lies in polishing and liberating and enabling those gifts [in others]."

Designated leaders are not always in the vanguard. An organization is fortunate to have pioneers in its ranks who are prepared to forge ahead. It is equally fortunate to be balanced by those who ask hard questions. Effective leaders draw the best from both and help the group to arrive at a decision.

The Content of Leadership

Leadership comes in many forms, even as leaders come in all sizes and shapes. The leader's style must be well matched to the needs of the organization. Robert Greenleaf has promoted servant leadership which seeks to fundamentally improve the caring quality of institutions through a new approach to leadership, structure, and decision-making. It is characterized by service to others, a holistic approach to work, and sharing power in decision-making. This is contrasted with a military style which can be appropriate and effective in crisis situations. Many leaders, servant or otherwise, use the charisma of their forceful personalities.

Personal style aside, John Kotter of the Harvard Business School, organizes the leadership task into three categories: visioning, aligning, and motivating.

Visioning

"Leaders need to have a sense of the unknowable and be able to see the unforeseeable," says Robert Greenleaf. They see the flower in the bud. They are on the cutting edge of tomorrow, pushing at the uncharted and the unknown. They are not content with the status quo.

Leaders are known for their creativity. Robert F. Kennedy enjoyed closing his campaign speeches by quoting Robert Frost, "Some men see things as they are and say 'why?' Others dream things that never were and say 'why not!'"

Many nonprofits, sadly, strive to give ever better administration to what amounts to second-rate ideas. They should heed Peter F. Drucker who said that effectiveness does not come from solving problems but from exploiting opportunities.

Leaders are risk-takers. After all the research has been done, after the wisest consultants have been heard, there remains a gap of uncertainty which can be bridged only by intuition and faith.

Visioning, like creativity, happens only in a receptive environment. Alexander Solzhenitsyn, the famous Soviet dissident, in his 1978 Harvard commencement address said, "Whenever the tissue of life is woven of legalistic relationships, this creates an atmosphere of spiritual mediocrity that paralyzes men's noblest impulses."

One of the boldest displays of visionary leadership I (Edgar) have witnessed occurred in January 1992 when Millard Fuller, president of Habitat for Humanity, proposed a plan to eradicate poverty housing in Sumter County, Georgia, by the year 2000. At the time, Habitat had bank loans into the millions of dollars, resulting from a temporary and serious shortfall in giving. The feasibility study which should precede such an effort had not been done. Satisfactory answers were not available to such basic questions as, How many houses will that take? Where will the money come from? Won't affiliates in other parts of the country object?

The board was understandably and maybe rightfully reluctant, but Millard was insistent. The proposition was finally approved with some qualifications after hours of debate. When the news reached Sumter County, of which Americus is the capital, it was greeted in the local newspapers with the biggest headlines since the end of World War II. A bold action begat a bold response as white churches, who had never supported Habitat before, formed partnerships with black churches to build houses. A businessman donated a valuable 30-acre tract of land for building sites. Businesses made donations and the project qualified for grants. Eighteen months later even the skeptics had been swept along by the momentum of this cause. It was so bold that it was crazy, but it is happening, and other communities are being inspired by the Sumter example.

Aligning

Guiding an action from the idea stage to an approved resolution requires skill and, what is commonly known as, statesmanship. All action starts with an idea which, in the early stages, is relatively simple. In the process of development, simple ideas often become incredibly complex. Justice Oliver Wendell Holmes said, "I would not give a fig for the simplicity this side of complexity, but I would give my life for simplicity on the other side of complexity."

Before an idea can be supported it must be understood. The sponsors of an idea must be prepared to explain it patiently and repeatedly. They must be able to articulate why it is needed and what it will accomplish. One very good way to do this is through a written proposal (see Chapter 7, The Doctrine of Completed Staff Work). In the alignment process, obstacles are negotiated, fears are assuaged and convictions are deepened. Everyone must be helped to develop commitment to the vision.

Motivating

The strongest motivating force is a compelling idea, well presented. Had Millard Fuller suggested that Habitat approve a watered-down version of what became the Sumter County Initiative, it would predictably have gotten a lukewarm response. Nonprofits need to continually coax themselves toward boldness.

It is dangerous to entrust a poignant idea to some people. They will either water it down to suit the most cautious constituent or make it so complex that people don't understand what they are being asked to support.

Early in my (Edgar) career, I worked for Orie O. Miller who was, in his day, probably the most dynamic leader in the Mennonite church. I noticed that when I left his office I was literally running. One day I said to myself, "Why are you running? A grown man, running down a public street?" Upon reflection I realized that Mr. Miller had so clarified the issue and made it seem so urgent that I could hardly wait to get back to the office to begin with its implementation.

The job market is prepared to pay the highest salaries for the gifts of leadership. Leaders rally the support of others. Leaders maximize opportunities. Effective organizations owe much to their leaders.

The Chair as Leader

Choosing a chairperson is an important decision. The chair must be well known and respected. She/he must understand the organization well and be dedicated to its mission. Her/his values must be consistent with those the board has identified for itself. Most of all she/he must be willing and able to make sufficient time available to serve in this capacity.

Some boards tend to elevate the person with most seniority or prestige to the chair position. Being an effective chair has little to do with either. Above all, the chair is expected to facilitate a group process which draws the best from individual members and the collective group.

The chair and the CEO stand at the most critical nexus of an organization. The chair is responsible for how the *board* functions, while the CEO is responsible for the effectiveness of the *administration*. How they perform individually, as well as the quality of their interaction, set the tone for the organization. An active chair performs many functions. We will identify four major ones.

Access to Information

The chair is responsible to ensure that the board has the information it needs to fulfill its role. The old computer term—garbage in, garbage out (GIGO)—applies. The administration or board committees should deliver quality reports on the agreed upon schedule ungrudgingly. Conversely, staff has a right to expect that their report will be read thoughtfully and without fail.

For many boards the problem is not so much the quantity of information—directors often complain about how much they are expected to read—but the right kind of information. Information should be well organized. It should be concise and available in sufficient time to be read in advance.

Boards should have access to some information which does not come through the staff filter. One of the major reports to come directly to the board is the annual audited report. Board members should visit project sites occasionally, but, in so doing, they should concentrate on Ends issues and not allow themselves to get drawn into administrative detail.

A Supportive Relationship with the CEO

A CEO is expected to support staff, but who supports and who maintains a supportive/supervisory relationship with the CEO? The chair. It is one of his/her most important non-meeting responsibilities. The two should meet regularly, at least once between meetings of the board, to talk about issues they face in their respective assignments. They should plan together and dream together. The fact of just being together, like at a sporting event, may serve the important purpose of deepening their relationship.

It would be highly unusual if these two strong individuals did not disagree on occasion. They can and they should. But the disagreement must be at the objective level. It cannot be allowed to disintegrate and become personal or acrimonious. Should this happen, the board must step in and resolve the problem. Protracted conflict can be very detrimental to everyone involved and must not be tolerated.

Quite apart from their personal compatibility, the chair and the CEO must have respect for the *office* of the other. An effective chair does not usurp the authority which is vested in the office of CEO and does not denigrate it in any way. The effective CEO humbly and joyfully submits him-/herself to the board to which he/she is accountable through the chair. There is no tug of war and no playing of games. The atmosphere is one of mutual respect and collaboration.

Preparing the Agenda

Since the chair is responsible for how the board functions, the chair is responsible for the agenda. This is contrary to the practice of many nonprofits where the agenda is drawn up by the CEO, and the chair reads it for the first time as she/he draws breath to call the meeting to order. The agenda is a plan for how the board spends its meeting time. It should be drawn up weeks before the meeting by the chair in consultation with the CEO and distributed to all who are expected to participate, along with the necessary background materials.

Conducting Meetings

Chairing is more than ceremony and formality. The criteria for a successful meeting is more than starting and adjourning meetings on time and conducting them according to Robert's Rules of Order. The crucial questions are, Were good decisions made? Was the mission furthered?

Anyone who accepts the responsibility of the chair surrenders some private prerogatives. One of these is to enter into vigorous debate on all the issues. A chair who is not able to restrain him-/herself in this way adds frustration to the process which he/she is expected to facilitate. Because of these limitations, some directors believe they can have more influence on the outcome of a meeting if they hold positions other than the chair.

The chair is expected to allocate the available meeting time so as to cover the entire agenda. This is not an easy task in a context where freedom of speech prevails. It happens (not infrequently!) that boards strain at a gnat (often at the top of the agenda) and end up swallowing camels (often late in the meeting).

Important as the office of chair is, all leaders need to be reminded that they are servants, accountable to those who elect them. Greenleaf says it, not once but twice, "No one, absolutely no one, is to be entrusted with the operational use of power without the close oversight of the fully functioning trustees. The enemy to effective leadership is strong natural servants who have the potential to lead but do not lead, or who choose to follow a non-servant."

Successful chairpersons are humbled by the responsibility which the office places on them. Lyndon B.

Johnson, not one of the humblest of men, said it well, "The presidency has made every man who occupied it, no matter how small, bigger than he was—and no matter how big, not big enough for its demands."

5.

MEETINGS:
Gain or Pain?

> "... For your meetings do more harm than good."
> —The Apostle Paul to the Corinthian Church
> in the New Testament

Meetings are a necessary part of organizational life. Organizations cannot exist without them. They can be, at the same time, an abysmal waste of time.

I (Edgar) was having a meeting in Paraguay when a man walked by and asked "What are they doing?" He was told that we were having a meeting. A puzzled look came over his face as he said incredulously, "Can't be—they are laughing!" Meetings in his mind where serious business!

We have all known staff persons who admit openly that board meetings are not their favorite activities. Some, in fact, find themselves with headaches, nervous stomachs, or other psychosomatic illnesses. This should not be so. If the board/administration partnership is what it should be, meetings should be productive and pleasant experiences.

We acknowledge at the outset that there are many different types of meetings. There are all-day board meetings with a full agenda, and there are special meetings which are called for a single purpose. A meeting may be for brainstorming, or it may be planned as a retreat.

Meetings take an enormous amount of time. A two-hour meeting of twenty people represents a full work week of 40 hours. To be productive, meetings should include the following:

- A clearly defined purpose
- Role assignments: chair, recorder, perhaps a timekeeper
- Agenda
- The transaction of business
- Clarification of future assignments
- Agreement on next meeting date, place, and agenda
- Evaluation

The success of a meeting depends more on the planning and preparation which precede it than it does on how the meeting is conducted. A poorly planned meeting cannot be conducted well. The key to successful meetings is planning.

Agenda Planning

The chair and the CEO jointly plan board meeting agendas. They should begin by identifying the priority items and issues and agree on how they are to be presented and by whom. If an issue is not yet at the proposal stage, it should be postponed. A time allotment should be made for each agenda item, and if the total exceeds the time available, adjustments must be made prior to the meeting accordingly. When completed, the agenda should be distributed to all participants well in advance of the meeting, along with clear instructions to the presenters. An agenda has the following components:

Meditation or Moment of Reflection: Directors are busy people. They leave demanding jobs and may jet to the meeting location, sometimes making telephone calls along the way. Upon arrival their bodies are present, but their minds may be elsewhere. As John Erskine described it, "The body travels more easily than the mind, and until we have limbered up our imaginations, we continue to think as though we had stayed home. We have not moved a step until we take up residency in someone else's point of view."

Some moments spent in quiet meditation and reflection can serve to unite the assembled group in spirit before the official deliberations begin. Even the U. S. Congress, with the vigilant American Civil Liberties Union looking over its shoulder, opens its daily sessions with prayer.

Review of agenda: This is an opportunity for the chair to supplement the written agenda with any further instructions. Board members can also satisfy themselves that issues they want to discuss are in the plan of the meeting.

Minutes of the previous meeting: Minutes should be distributed soon after a meeting. If this is done, it is necessary only to review the weightier actions and to give an opportunity for additions or corrections. If a board meets infrequently, minutes serve as a good review. (For a fuller discussion of minutes, see Chapter 6, Minutes.)

Reports: Staff and committee reports should have been distributed and read in advance of the meeting. A good report anticipates the questions which are in the minds of directors and answers them before they are asked. Once the main activities have been reported on, the directors should have a relatively clear understanding of how things are going and should be prepared to address the business of the meeting.

Old business: This is business which has been tabled at a previous meeting or carried over for whatever reason. It should be dealt with before turning to the new business of the day.

New business: This is the heart of the meeting. Housekeeping business has been completed, and now the board is free to address the major issues which will serve to further the mission. This includes planning, evaluating, and processing proposals. Meeting planners must exercise discipline to insure that this valuable time does not get compromised by less important, but apparently more urgent, business.

Executive sessions: There should be opportunity for a board to meet in executive session with only members of the board in attendance. Executive sessions should not be reserved for crisis issues only. Confidential issues should be discussed in a closed session, although we discuss some precautions about this procedure in Chapter 9, Information.

Summary: We like the tradition of those boards who reserve some time at the end of the meeting for everyone to express a concluding comment. It is a way of gathering useful information which would otherwise go unexpressed, particularly from members who have not entered fully into the discussion.

Next meeting date: Before adjournment, the next meeting time and place should be set. It is, in fact, good to set meeting dates for an entire year or more. It is also advisable to identify topics which are to receive major attention at the next meeting and to make assignments. This practice helps to carry the momentum of one meeting to the next.

Evaluation: If not at every meeting, then at least annually, board members should have an opportunity to comment on how meetings are organized and conducted. If a chair truly seeks to facilitate a collective process, he/she will want to know the level of satisfaction and solicit suggestions for improvement.

Distributing the Meeting Time

Meeting time is always limited. It must be allocated judiciously in keeping with the priorities of the meeting. A board may set up a rotation to give in-depth attention to a different program division at each meeting.

A board benefits by periodically analyzing how it allocates its time. Many boards are startled to discover how much time they spend on hearing reports and how little on planning for the future. Planning often appears at the end of the agenda, after the routine business has been done. Too often most meeting time is given to hearing reports and wrestling with immediate problems, leaving little, if any, time for future planning. This tendency can only be corrected by thoroughly preparing and informing board members in advance of the meeting, by intentionally organizing the agenda, and by deliberately conducting the meeting so that planning time is preserved. The following brief exercise may prove to be revealing.

FIGURE 4

Allocation of Board Meeting Time

Activity	Time Presently Spent	What Should it be?
Reports (past)	%	%
Problem-Solving (present)	%	%
Planning (future)	%	%
Total	**100%**	**100%**

Protracted and inconclusive debate should not be permitted. Beyond a certain point, in the words of an experienced chair, there is "nothing new but more of it."

The role of the chair in such situations is to collect the concerns in writing so the presenter has them for reference when rewriting the proposal. Sometimes it is useful to grant a period for cooling off, for reflecting, and for gathering additional information. In all situations, efforts must be made to respect the rest of the agenda.

Meeting Ground Rules

Every board of directors must decide what rules will govern its meetings. Will the meetings be bound by Robert's Rules of Order? The rules produced by Major Robert more than one hundred years ago have been widely recognized as a workable procedure by which many meetings are conducted. They have their value, to be sure, but they are, in the minds of some, more appropriate for the U. S. House of Representatives than for nonprofit board meetings.

Meetings must allow the group to deliberate in an orderly fashion and to carry through its will. The procedure by which this is accomplished should be appropriate to the size of the group and the wishes of the membership. A procedure which is unduly technical can be intimidating to persons who have not mastered Robert's Rules. Excessive legalism, too, can be a form of obstruction or manipulation on the part of a leader.

The Role of Debate and Dissent

Healthy organizations allow—even welcome— differing points of view. In a pluralistic society, it is said, where five people are present, there are six points of view. That need not be bad. Most ideas can benefit from processing. Few ideas, it seems, fall from heaven fully developed.

Ideas originate in creative minds, often in response to something which needs to be improved. They are refined in debate, and in this process they also become owned.

Only ideas which can survive vigorous analysis deserve to be adopted.

A word of caution is, however, in order. Some organizational environments are so hostile to new ideas that they need protection. New ideas, like spring flowers, are tender and easily trampled. They must be thoughtfully presented.

There is room for an honest difference of opinion on many subjects, but our experience is that most prolonged and heated debate is the result of deficiencies in presentation and pre-meeting preparation. It should not be necessary to use board meeting time to refine a proposal and to clarify what was intended.

When the essential facts are on the table and there is a seriously divided opinion, the board has several options. If the issue is not urgent it can be tabled, allowing for study or rewriting. If meeting time permits, an effort can be made to arrive at a collaborative conclusion (see Chapter 12, Conflict). As a last resort, it is always possible to revert to a "majority rules" position. An organization must be able to arrive at a timely decision. Meeting times and energy are limited. The tendency to draw back from a difficult decision is ever present.

I (Edgar) was presiding over the Habitat board when there was heated and protracted debate over a recommendation to purchase and renovate an old building to serve as the corporate headquarters. The facts had been well presented and the board was seriously divided. At any given time there were three to five directors waiting their turn to speak. Suddenly it dawned on me that this could come down to the vote of the chair, as the body seemed evenly divided. I favored the resolution, but, had it come down to my vote, I would have voted against it on the principle that an action of this importance did not deserve to pass with a majority of one.

Dissent serves a purpose. Organizations should not run over it lightly or regard the dissenter as an enemy. Organizations need members who have the strength of their convictions. No one has said it better than St. Thomas Aquinas: "We love them both, those whose opinions we share and those whose opinions we reject. For both have labored in the search for truth and both have helped in the finding of it."

A Meeting Ethic

One of the bad habits boards fall into is to talk about people in their absence. I (Edgar) once participated in a meeting when the work of an absent member was referred to critically. A new member asked with an inflection of surprise, "Do we criticize someone in their absence?" In a soft but unapologetic voice he added, "I'd rather not."

We all had been addressed. Our new member had introduced a meeting ethic which has made our communication more honest. No longer are people spoken about. They are spoken to, and that has both raised the ethical tone of our meetings and has made our communications more effective.

Brainstorming

Organizations must push themselves to get beyond housekeeping routines, to spend time thinking and dreaming about the future. A special retreat-type meeting may be called for this purpose, or time may be reserved in a regular meeting.

Brainstorming can be viewed as a mental walkabout. To be effective, the subject to be brainstormed should be carefully selected and clearly focused. Open-ended issues which are provocative and issues surrounding change are best. For example, how can we attract more young people into our program? Brainstorming should be guided by the following ground rules:

• The leader announces the subject and reminds everyone that all ideas are welcome. Nothing is irrelevant or impossible!

• Humor and wild ideas are encouraged. The leader's remarks should relax the usual inhibitions. The time limit usually can be short and should certainly not exceed one hour. No distinction is made between board and staff contributions.

• An understanding is reached on what is to be done with the results. The two obvious options are:

—interesting, but no further action is needed.

—assigned for further development.

• A recorder is appointed to list the ideas exactly as presented on a blackboard or flip chart. No attempts should be made to challenge or even to clarify them.

• Everybody is expected to contribute. There are no spectators. Contributions driven by passion are permissible.

• Long speeches are not permitted. Short sound-bites are preferred.

The greatest value of a brainstorming session is that directors give themselves permission to think new, even daring, thoughts. It gets the organization's adrenalin flowing. Even as good photographers are willing to take one hundred pictures to get five or ten useful ones, so organizational leaders must be willing to sort through dozens of ideas before they find one that is deserving of their time.

Frequency of Meetings

A board needs to decide how frequently it wants to meet. The board of a young organization, whose members are local, may meet monthly, whereas the board of an older organization, whose members are scattered nationally or even internationally, may meet quarterly or semi-annually. Large boards, whose members come from a wide geographical spread, may meet annually, but have an active Executive Committee in place.

Our preference is "not too often and not too long." A board that meets frequently predictably spends time on Means rather than Ends issues. It may be managing and not leading.

Long board meetings (for me [Edgar], anything after 10:00 p.m. is long) should not be necessary when the "doctrine of completed staff work" is adhered to (see Chapter 7) and when the meeting is well conducted.

Trees, we are told, die from the top down. The same is true of organizations. When a board is functioning well, as reflected in the quality of its meetings, chances are that the whole organization is functioning well. When an organization consistently has poor meetings, it is a sign of trouble. Meetings are a reflection of the organization. Good organizations have good meetings. Good meetings eventually result in good organizations.

6.

MINUTES:
More Than a Formality

> *"Not seconds, and not hours—MINUTES!"*
>
> —Chet Raber

Approving the minutes has become such a perfunctory function that it would be easy to conclude that minutes are an unimportant formality. Few things could be further from the truth.

Minutes serve as the memory of an organization. Anybody wanting to know what an organization was doing ten years ago, or fifty years ago, should be able to trace it through the minute record. The ability to look back gives an organization perspective. It makes it possible to trace trends and growth. Meeting recorders should understand their work from both the legal and the historical perspective.

Minutes are also the official record of a board's actions. Once approved, minutes become a part of the official record. Directors who vote against an action which is adopted have a right to ask that their vote be recorded. The legal function of minutes is discussed more fully in Chapter 13.

Minutes should record where and when the meeting

took place, who was present and absent, and who the officers were. Most of all, minutes should record what was decided and the factors which led to the final conclusion. The latter is important for absent members and for the record. Minutes should be written so that they are comprehensible to someone who was not present at the meeting. Significant papers may be attached to the minute record, thus preserving the content without much additional effort, while keeping the body of minutes shorter.

Responsibility for the minute record is usually assigned in the bylaws to the secretary. Boards who work fast find that appointing a staff assistant to assist in minute-keeping facilitates the process and, at the same time, permits the board secretary to also participate in the discussion. Laptop word processors are increasingly finding their way into the boardroom. They are ideal for keeping good records.

Organizations develop their own minute-writing style. Giving minutes titles and numbers is helpful for easy reference and cataloging. Following is an illustration which we consider to be a good minute format:

#14 BUDGET APPROVAL: The proposed budget was presented by Tom Brown, chairperson of the Finance Committee, assisted by Controller Nancy Smith, along with the current budget and a projection of the financial trends of the current year. (A copy of their presentation is attached to the minutes.) Brown and Smith observed that the proposed budget calls for a 5% increase in income and assured the Board that this is within the guidelines it had established in its previous meeting. Numerous questions were asked about anticipated income sources and proposed spending adjustments. The Board was assured that increases in the pension policy have been factored into the proposed budget.

When all questions had been answered, it was moved, seconded, and passed that the annual budget be approved as presented with the understanding that giving trends be kept under close review. If income falls behind expenditures, staff is asked to recommend a plan to bring the budget back in balance.

Recording a discussion or brainstorming meeting, as contrasted with a "business meeting," requires a special approach. It is important that such contributions be well recorded. A day's work can easily be lost by an incompetent recorder. Writing ideas on a blackboard or newsprint can help to facilitate and focus discussion. A skillful recorder can sharpen the conclusions beyond the meeting itself. Capturing the essence of an extended discussion in writing is a valuable gift.

Minutes should be available in draft form days after a meeting. They should then be approved by the secretary and the chair and distributed soon after the meeting. Board members should read them immediately and promptly call any additions or corrections to the attention of the secretary. Minutes which have been distributed in advance do not need to be read at the meeting, although minutes are official only after they have been approved.

7.

THE DOCTRINE
of Completed Staff Work

> *"No presente problemas, soluciones."*
> *(Don't present problems; solutions.)*
> — A Spanish proverb

Issues must be well thought through and processed before they are presented to the board for action. "No raw meat," we say. "Everything must be pre-cooked."

It may sound simple, but it is not easy and is often violated. Inadequate meeting preparation probably contributes more to long and bungled meetings, poor decisions, and low director morale than any other single thing. This can be corrected, and board effectiveness and efficiency can be improved.

A weak or an inexperienced executive or committee chair may describe an idea or a problem to the board in a general way, ending with, What do you think? What should we do? He folds his hands into his lap and assumes that he has done his job. But instead of leading the board and facilitating the process, he has presented it with several problems.

To take a raw idea or problem and prepare it for board action in the form of a written proposal takes time and requires some effort and skill. This work must be done by staff or committee before the meeting. The board should resolutely refuse to spend time on issues which have not been properly prepared in advance.

Proposal Development

Proposals are the link between an idea and action. They come in response to either a problem or an opportunity. Written proposals prepare an idea in such a manner that its merits can be evaluated. Leadership is expressed through proposals.

The seminal idea, which is the core of a proposal, can originate with any person at any time. Regardless of its origin, its merits must be carefully and respectfully evaluated. Some ideas, for a variety of valid reasons, never make the grade. Most ideas are substantially changed while they are developing. An idea under serious consideration should be expressed in the form of a written proposal so that it can be carefuly evaluated. A well prepared proposal must include the following information:

1. **Who** is making the proposal?
2. **To whom** is it addressed?
3. **When** is it being made?
4. **What** is being proposed? (For example, it may be a plan to expand fund raising.)
5. **Why** is the proposed action needed? Identify the problem or the opportunity which is calling for the proposed action.
6. **What** will it accomplish? State the specific goals and relate them to the organization's mission.
7. **What** will it cost? Capital expenditures? Projected first-year operating cost? Projected five-year operating cost? (The cost should be related to the projected benefits.)
8. **Where** is this activity to take place?

9. **When** will it be implemented? When will it be evaluated? What is the intended duration of this activity?

10. **List several alternatives** which have been carefully considered and eliminated for whatever reason. Listing questions remaining to be explored reveals the incompleteness of a proposal but may add comprehensiveness and credibility to a proposal.

Seldom should a proposal exceed one or two pages in length, although it can be supplemented by attachments.

A proposal is not ready for board action until it has been cleared by all who are directly implicated by it. Staff members or other board committees who are affected by a proposal should be consulted before it is presented to the board for action. For example, the financial implications of a proposal are related to the budget and should be discussed with the finance committee or department in advance. The same principle applies to staffing or other implications.

What if staff or the sponsoring board committee are not of one mind regarding the merits or content of a proposal? We believe that the proposal is then not yet ready for presentation. But, in the end, if not everyone can agree but the proposal has substantial support, it should be presented with a brief but fair reference to the dissenting points of view. The final decision belongs with the board. If the proposal is approved, everyone, supporters and dissenters alike, should work together to put it into action.

Board Options

A board is expected to examine new proposals vigorously. An idea which cannot survive critical examination does not deserve to be adopted. Having completed its review, a board of directors has one of three options:

1. **Approve:** Before a proposal is approved it belongs

to the presenter(s). It has no official status. Once approved, it belongs to the organization who is responsible for it. The enabling minute should delegate responsibility for its implementation. Conditions attached to the approval should be stated clearly.

2. **Disapprove:** The board may feel that the proposal is not within the organization's mission, or that funding or staffing are not available. Directors should not give their approval against their better judgment.

3. **Amend:** A board has the prerogative to scale a proposal up or down or to amend it in whatever way it chooses. It should, however, not allow itself to be drawn into a time-consuming exercise. If the amendments are major, the proposal should be tabled and rescheduled for the next meeting. Hasty approval often results in unnecessary problems and complications later.

A board is rightfully judged by the quality of its decisions. Good decisions are based on carefully gathered and presented information. Practicing the doctrine of completed staff (and committee) work increases organizational effectiveness. It raises morale and fosters a spirit of teamwork.

8.

MONEY:
It Makes the World Go Round

> *"The ultimate question, which I think people in the nonprofit organization should be asking again and again and again, both of themselves and of the institution, is: 'What should I hold myself accountable for by way of contribution and results? What should this institution hold itself accountable for by way of contribution and results? What should this institution and I be remembered for?'"*
>
> — Peter F. Drucker

A friend, who was the best treasurer an organization could wish to have, was fond of saying, "Money isn't everything, but it sure beats whatever is in second place." Spoken as a true treasurer? Perhaps, but try running an organization without money, or with too little money! It changes everything. Ultimately, in our world, things have a way of needing money.

Many nonprofit organizations are firm in their belief that their workers, the volunteers, are their most valued resource. But even volunteers cost money, and when there isn't enough of it, their number is reduced and their effectiveness is hindered. The important role money plays in the life of an organization cannot be denied.

There are, when you stop to think of it, four things organizations do with money:

1) They earn it, through fees for services.

2) They raise it, by inviting others to support their cause.

3) They spend it in the furtherance of their mission.

4) If some is left over temporarily, and there should be, they can store it for later use.

In truth, there is yet a fifth thing organizations do with money. They waste it. Their biggest waste is probably not in poor purchasing practices or in frivolity but in supporting undeserving causes, in tolerating inefficiency, and in losing opportunities.

Earning Money

Many organizations derive a significant portion of their operating budgets from fees for services. This includes hospitals, retirement homes, parochial schools, camps, and mutual insurance companies. Such organizations need to put a fair price on their services and be businesslike in their procedures.

Raising Money

If governments get their power from their ability to tax, nonprofits get power from their ability to raise contributions. An organization can achieve its mission only if it has a sound financial base.

We have all known organizations who exaggerate their accomplishments. They are sometimes described as organizations with a six-foot whistle and a six-inch boiler.

It is true, at the same time, that many organizations do not know how to present their work in ways that attract the public support they need and deserve. They are a light under a bushel. Organizations which thrive have both an effective program and a compelling way of presenting it.

An increasingly skeptical public withholds its support when it is not convinced that an organization has made a serious commitment to quality and excellence. Before organizations mount fund-raising drives, they should ask themselves what they have to offer and whether they are presenting it in a convincing manner.

Board members should contribute to causes they direct. This is not to suggest that the biggest contributors should automatically be elected to the board, but directors are expected to contribute in proportion to their means.

An organization we know discovered that not all of its directors were making an annual contribution, and so the subject was discussed by the board. As a result, they adopted a clear statement which said that in the future all board members were expected to contribute annually. Not only did giving increase, but directors also became noticeably more enthusiastic and involved. The leadership example of the board strengthened the base for future fund-raising campaigns.

Directors are expected to help with fund raising. In small organizations directors frequently raise all or most of the necessary funds. When an organization reaches a certain size, staff is retained for this function, but directors should give their active support to the fund-raising effort.

Not only are directors responsible to ensure that sufficient funds are available, they are also responsible for *how* funds are raised in the name of the organization. An organization's public image is shaped in large measure by *how* it raises and spends its money.

The public is preoccupied with overhead costs and rightly so. Many nonprofits have not proven themselves to be deserving of the public trust. Yet all organizations have overhead. We would not support one which pretends not to have overhead. Nor should it be assumed that organizations which claim to have the lowest overhead are automatically the most efficient. An alert nonprofit board keeps its overhead ratio under constant review and keeps it below industry or association averages.

Spending Money

Organizations reveal their true character by how they spend their money. Those with integrity concentrate their resources on their mission. Most organizations plan this through the budgeting process which serves the following functions:

1. A budget is, first of all, an incontrovertible statement of the organization's priorities and mission. A mission statement, valuable as it is, is words. It may or may not reflect accurately what an organization does. Anybody wanting to know what an organization is doing should examine its budget.

2. A budget is a plan which projects anticipated income and expenses before the year begins. If income and expenses are not in balance, ways must be found to either increase income or reduce expenses, or both. Wise budget-planning avoids the herky-jerky effect which results from the irregular availability of funds which is so disruptive to good performance.

3. Finally, budget approval is important as an authorization process. When a budget is approved, the items in it should be looked upon as authorized. This is why approving the annual budget is one of the most defining and "owning" actions that a board takes.

Individual organizations evolve their own budgeting format. As in so many other areas, a middle ground must be found between a format which is so detailed as to be cumbersome and one which is so brief as to be meaningless.

A common mistake organizations make is to commit all of their anticipated income early in the year, leaving no room for crises or opportunities which arise in the course of the year. Some correct this through approving a relatively large contingency fund for appropriation throughout the year.

Thinking in one-year blocks is another organizational error. Long-term programs should not be operated on a series of one-year plans. As when driving a car, it is a good practice for directors to concentrate not only on the immediate, but also to scan the horizon.

A clear policy should exist about how much latitude staff has to move money from one budget category to another without approval.

Before concluding this section on budgets, we recognize a corrective offered by John Carver in his book, *Boards That Make a Difference.* Carver believes that in their predisposition to fall into the Means rut, boards spend too much time on budgets. Budgets, he believes, are primarily an administrative tool and, therefore, belong primarily to the administration. This may be the case for organizations which are very mature. It is our belief that for organizations in Stages I-V, approving the annual budget is one of the most important actions a board takes.

Storing Money (Balances)

Increasingly, organizations need to have balances or reserves to carry them across lean times. Income for most nonprofits seldom comes in a steady stream which neatly matches expenditures. Organizations must have ways of managing those peaks and valleys so that programs do not suffer from seasonal fluctuation.

Not only does income vary seasonally, some projects are oversubscribed, while others have less appeal. This was true, for example, in 1992 when Habitat for Humanity received more than $5 million in response to the devastation of Hurricane Andrew. Organizations must have procedures to hold balances which have been designated until good program is in place to use them. Donors have the right to expect that their designations will be respected.

Accountability

Nonprofits are by definition public, not private, organizations. Directors have both a moral and a legal responsibility to live up to their public trust. Trust is one of an organization's most valuable assets. Financial accountability is therefore one of a board's most important and non-delegable tasks.

Most board decisions are based on reports which are prepared by the administration. The board is responsible to approve the reporting format and the schedule by which reports are to be supplied. The formats should be understandable by directors who are not professional accountants and should permit the directors to monitor in major categories the income and expenses for both the reporting period (frequently a month) and the year-to-date. Included should be comparisons to the monthly and year-to-date plans and the corresponding period of the previous year. The administration should comply with the agreed-upon reporting schedule without fail.

The board may additionally want to appoint a finance committee, to be composed of directors who have expertise in this area, who will analyze activity in greater depth and lead the board in this area of its responsibility.

All organizations, regardless of size, should have an annual audit. Audits are always addressed to the board, not to the CEO, because financial accountability is finally *board* responsibility. A newly elected director should ask to see the latest audited report. Any recommendations, and surely "reportable conditions"(or misdeeds), should receive prompt and decisive attention.

Some small and very young nonprofits find it hard to justify the cost of a professional audit. Minimally, such an organization should invite a committee composed of persons with good financial reputations to review the records, verify bank balances, and render a written report of their findings.

Audits normally cover only the financial activity at the headquarters level. They do not reach down to the levels within the organization where much of the financial activity takes place. This calls for a system of *internal* audits. For example, the Mennonite Central Committee, a world relief organization, is audited at the headquarters level by a professional public accounting firm. It additionally assigns staff auditors to perform *field* audits. This procedure extends a system of formal accountability throughout the entire organization.

Financial oversight is a major board responsibility. Board members should review financial statements conscientiously, along with program activities, to make sure the organization is performing its mission and meeting its ongoing responsibilities.

Nonprofit directors should also be knowledgeable about purchasing managers' insurance, bonding, etc. These issues are discussed in more detail in Chapter 13, Legal Dimensions. Directors should also avail themselves of books and professional advice on such subjects.

What Is the Bottom Line When There Is No "Bottom Line"?

This is a chapter title in Peter F. Drucker's book, *Managing The Nonprofit Organization: Principles and Practices.* Drucker reminds us that "performance is the ultimate test of any institution." Then he points out that "nonprofit institutions tend not to give priority to performance or results." Nonprofits are tempted to make their case by expounding on their good intentions or through obligating donors by pleading poverty rather than by demonstrating results. The results in a nonprofit that really count, let us be reminded, are those that benefit the clients of the organization.

Corporations are commonly criticized for being excessively preoccupied with the bottom line. But the bottom line, coupled with the need to have a competitively priced product, gives corporations a focus and drives them to efficiency for which nonprofits do not have an equivalent. We say, reluctantly but in truth, that we have seen long-term nonprofit employees who do not know the value of a dollar.

The public is rightfully skeptical of do-gooders who end up accomplishing very little good. The board of Habitat for Humanity has a need to know how many houses are being built. The American Bible Society has a need to know how many Scriptures are being translated and distributed. The Girl Scouts of America has a need to know how many girls are participating in their program and if, in the long run, scouting makes a difference in their lives.

9.

INFORMATION:
The Need to Know

> *"Information free from interest or prejudice, free from the vanity of the writer or the influence of the government, is as necessary to the human mind as pure air and water to the body."*
> —William Rees-Mogg, Editor, *London Times*

The public has an almost insatiable *desire* to know. *The New York Times* offers us "all the news that's fit to print." Our society functions on information. We have newspapers, magazines, and books galore. We have telephones, television, photocopiers, computers, and fax machines. We have weather reports and market reports. We want information that affects us instantly.

We also have a *right* to know. Information affects us, whether it is a scandal in city hall, a bomb scare, or a threatening tornado. Information empowers.

We act on information available to us. For example, once the public was convinced that pollution was a serious global environmental problem, many of us adopted less wasteful lifestyles. Today recycling programs are broadly supported.

To function well, organizations need to dispense information. Much information is a matter of public record.   Organizations are rightfully expected to make annual financial statements available.   Public appeals must include some disclosure.

Organizations which are generous in sharing non-confidential information earn the loyalty and support of their publics.   Organizations which share information grudgingly call suspicion on themselves. Employees have a right and a need to be informed at a level beyond the public.

How an organization handles information says a lot about it.   In a healthy organization, information flows freely and accurately to everyone who has a right to know. An unhealthy organization is composed of a network of cliques.   Information flows selectively and gets embellished along the way.   Gossip is the everyday word that describes this dynamic.

Organizations contribute to a gossip mentality by attempting to be too secretive.   We say, "attempting," because most systems "leak," and when basic facts aren't made available through legitimate channels, imaginations and speculation go to work.   Rumor is, in most cases, worse than fact.

The best leaders are surprisingly open in their manner. Guarding information excessively hints of insecurity and arrogance.

Information Carries Responsibility with It

The question Senator Howard Baker asked repeatedly at the Watergate hearings was, "What did he (President Nixon) know and when did he know it?"   Consumer warning labels and tornado alerts assume that people are responsible to act on information available to them.

Directors have both a need and a right to know.   They can't and don't need to know everything, but there should be agreement with the administration about what information will be routinely available and an understanding that no information will be deliberately withheld from them. Dr. David Hubbard, President of Fuller Theological Seminary, says, "We have a policy to tell bad news at 110% and good news at 90% in order to compensate for the tendency to cheat." Once information is in the hands of directors, they are responsible to act on it. Information carries with it the responsibility to act.

It is more difficult for directors to decide what to do with unfavorable information they receive about their organization through nonofficial channels. They have an obvious responsibility to hear it. They can and should ask some follow-up questions to determine the veracity of the allegation. Preposterous information should obviously be dismissed, but what if it appears to be plausible? There are several things directors in this position should *not* do:

1. They should not take unofficial and unsubstantiated information at face value. They should not be quick to believe the worst. They should assume an "innocent until proven guilty" stance.

2. They should not launch into their own unauthorized investigation. If they do so, they may add credence to what may only be a rumor.

3. They most assuredly should not confront an accused individual. Doing so would be indiscreet and could inflict unnecessary hurt.

4. They should not ignore it and wish it would all go away. Even unsubstantiated information carries with it responsibility.

What should directors do? They should report what they have been told to the board chair promptly and accurately. Then they should draw back and talk to no one about it. The responsibility now rests with the chair. The chair may already know about it, and corrective action may be under way. They may decide together that the issue does not deserve further processing. The chair may wish to discuss the issue with the CEO. The directors may want to check back after some weeks, and if they are not satisfied with what has been done, they should not hesitate to bring it up again. In an extreme case, they might even insist on bringing it to the board in a closed session.

The Need for Confidentiality

Not everybody can know everything. Not everybody *needs* to know everything. Confidentiality is necessary at all levels within an organization. Some information is not for public consumption, at least not immediately. The residents of a nursing home, for example, have a right to expect that information pertaining to their personal health will not become street talk. Banks and insurance companies possess information that must be kept confidential. Ministers and executives are trusted with information that must not be passed on. Journalists have the legal right to protect the sources of their information. Much information, including employee references, is gathered with a promise of confidentiality.

Processing confidential information usually involves informing other people. The circle of knowing widens. The concern is how to do so responsibly. The decision to share sensitive information must pass a three-point test:

1. **Necessity:** Is there a *need* to know?

2. **Competence:** The informant must be convinced that the listener is competent to handle the information professionally and maturely.

3. **Altruism:** The informant must feel confident that the listener will not use the information for her or his personal benefit or revenge.

Lapses in confidentiality have both practical and legal implications. Broken confidences create ill will and break trust which is hard to rebuild.

Legal Responsibility

Board members need to be reminded that on some issues, legal responsibility overrides regular procedure, including confidentiality. A board member, for example, who has information to suggest that a staff member is engaging in child abuse is legally obligated to report it to the chair, and they should together consult with the CEO. If there is an attempt by others in the organization to circumvent legal responsibilities, the board member who first learned of the problem is obligated to report it, regardless of the consequences.

Closed Sessions

A board has both a right and a need to meet in private with only board members present, and it should do so regularly, not only in crisis situations. Certain information must be guarded, and some organizational procedures are best conducted in a less public setting. This includes disciplinary action, salary issues, and board debate on sensitive and/or personal issues. Soliciting the opinions of directors before conducting an evaluation of the CEO's performance is best done in a closed session.

The whole tenor of a meeting changes when the doors close. Directors who were too timid to speak before, or who spoke in a very veiled way, suddenly come alive. The discussion may advance quickly from established facts to speculation. Unless some discipline is imposed, an executive session can deteriorate quickly into irresponsible gossip. Executive sessions are nevertheless necessary and can produce good results when three features are incorporated into the process:

1. **A resolute search for the truth.** Directors do well to remember the warning of U.N. Secretary General Dag Hammarskjöld that persons who judge on the basis of one-sided facts are by definition unjust. The pursuit of justice must include a willingness to hear both sides before forming an opinion. It is never easy to sort fact from fiction, but wise and just decisions cannot be based on speculation and unfounded accusations. If the facts available are not adequate to conclude a matter, the discussion should be tabled until more information can be gathered. Going beyond the facts is not only counterproductive, it is dangerous. Closing the doors is not a license for irresponsible behavior.

2. **Involve the person(s) implicated as much as possible.** Speaking *with* someone is always preferred to speaking *about* them. Before closing the doors, a board would be wise to ask itself what it is shutting in and what it is shutting out. In one such situation where I (Edgar) was involved, the facts had long since been exhausted and the meeting continued mostly on hearsay and speculation. When the person who was the subject of the discussion was finally permitted to speak on his own behalf, everyone saw quickly how incomplete the information was and how unfair the accusations. The meeting had been largely unproductive.

3. **Determine that the issue is ready for a board airing.** If a grievance is involved, has it gone through the board-approved grievance procedure? If it is a very personal issue, sometimes a pre-meeting with a smaller group is more appropriate. Often a meeting takes place before the facts have been adequately gathered. When a meeting takes place before the facts have been gathered and the best alternatives identified, it is likely to inflict more pain than it will produce gain.

Once a conclusion has been reached, the person affected should be informed immediately and directly. Sometimes it is helpful to do this in the presence of all who participated in the decision. At the least, the person should be told who helped make the decision. A board must be willing to own its decisions and face people who are negatively affected by them, regardless of how uncomfortable that may be. Boards, for all their power, sometimes act in a surprisingly cowardly fashion.

We have both been on both sides of the closed door. We know how easy it is to be paranoid when on the outside and how easy it is to feel smug when on the inside. We know the dangers but also the need for a board to meet regularly, though not necessarily at length, in private. Closed sessions are, we are convinced, necessary and can serve a useful purpose if properly conducted.

Managing information wisely is an important organizational function. Effective communication is a discipline in its own right. Beware of the organization that hides behind anonymity and revels in secrecy.

10.

CONSULTANTS:
Helping Boards to Help Themselves

> *"In dealing with experts, we may fear showing our ignorance (even though we may be entitled to it). We may also be afraid to put ourselves somewhat at the expert's mercy. Moreover, an expert often uncovers more problems than he solves. He may force us to focus on issues that we were able to ignore before."*
> —Roger A. Golde in *Muddling Through*

Organizations are occasionally confronted with problems which leave them baffled. It may be something internal, such as need for a reorganization brought on by growth or the retirement of a key employee, or it may be due to the introduction of a new service or technology. In either case, an organization may be like a sailboat. The boat is beautiful, the rigging is fine, the view is excellent, but the boat can't move, or it is moving very slowly. Staff and board have tinkered but can't seem to find the combination which permits the organization to benefit from the gentle breeze. Sometimes a relatively minor consultation can produce surprising results.

Some organizations use consultants even when there is no major problem. They find that the participation of an outside person provides perspective on their unique mission and opportunities.

Directors are sometimes reluctant to engage a consultant because they see it as a sign of weakness, or it confronts them with something unpleasant which they are trying to ignore. Once the urgency is great enough to push them beyond this point they become skeptical. "How can someone, who doesn't know our business nearly as well as we, solve our problems? And what is more, consultants are expensive."

Are they? What is the value of helping an organization get over an obstacle or meet a new challenge? The cost/benefit ratio of using a well selected consultant can be very favorable.

I (Chet) was contacted by the chair of a board dissatisfied with the results of its organization. He found communication with the CEO to be difficult. Employees, as well, were expressing dissatisfaction with management.

Within a few sessions the board became able to address each of its concerns. The board initiated two meetings per month between the board chair and the CEO to discuss the ongoing work of the organization and board/CEO relationships. Policies for the organization were developed, including that of the relationship of the CEO to the board. An annual performance plan for the CEO with specific goals was instituted. And, critically, the principle was established that all decisions would come to either the board or management by way of proposals.

Changes of this nature do not occur overnight, but within a short time significant positive results had occurred. The relationship between the board and CEO, and between management and employees, was considerably improved. Long-term targets for change were set in place. All participants seemed well satisfied with the direction and the immediate results. They look forward to the longer-term results of a more organized, confident, and clearly run organization.

For Whom Does a Consultant Work?

Do consultants work for the board or the CEO? The answer is either or both. When the issues being examined are board issues—for example, board organization and structure, philosophy of management, or strategic planning—the consultant works directly with and for the board. If the subjects of concentration are management related, the consultant may work for the CEO.

When a consultant works directly with the board, it may be threatening to the CEO. A wise consultant will maintain good linkage with all persons needed to insure the success of a consultation.

Practical Steps in Engaging a Consultant

The effectiveness of a consultation can be materially enhanced by adhering to the following suggestions:

1. **Describing the assignment.** What is the consultant expected to do? Answering this question well is the most important and difficult part of the assignment. The assignment should be described in writing and negotiated with the consultant until expectations are clear. It is not uncommon for assignment descriptions to go through multiple drafts. Proceeding without such an understanding is like committing to a trip without agreeing on a destination.

2. **Selecting the consultant.** There are many good consultants, but a consultant can do a good job only if she or he is relevant to the need. An expert is expert only in her or his field of expertise. Before a consultant is engaged, it is advisable to review a list of clients, present or past, and get references from two or three.

3. **Agreeing on charges and timetable.** When will the work begin and when will it be completed? What are the charges, and when is payment to be made?

4. **Meeting regularly.** Consultants work best when they are in regular communication with the persons for whom they are working. Regular interaction is required to keep the assignment focused and to exchange pertinent information. If a consultant is being engaged to do a one-day seminar, those responsible should ask to review the preparation in advance of the meeting. The contribution of a consultation is better when the client is part of the process.

5. **Preparing to act on the consultant's recommendations.** Consultants do not make decisions on behalf of their clients. At best they help them to see the available alternatives and potential consequences. A consultation is not complete until those who commissioned it have discussed the conclusions thoroughly and thoughtfully and made provision for their implementation.

At this point the board is again confronted with the hard decisions which called for the consultation in the first place. Now, hopefully, the board has information which make the decisions easier. Failure to properly process a consultant's recommendations renders the effort a waste of money and opportunity.

Consultants can be viewed as regular employees, with one exception. Their employment is temporary. Consultants perform best when they are integrated into the ongoing process, when they are able to get well acquainted with the people for whom and with whom they are working, when communication between consultant and client is open.

Good consultants do not call attention to themselves or try to take a lot of credit for their work. Their satisfaction comes in knowing that they had a part in solving a problem or in recognizing an opportunity. They do not overwhelm; they empower. The best consultants can be described by the Chinese proverb, "When their task is accomplished, their work is done, the people will remark: 'We have done it ourselves.'"

11.

PLANNING

> *"Planning should be reality based and vision driven."*
> —Richard Celeste, Ohio Governor 1983-91,
> Habitat for Humanity International Board Member

The best nonprofit leaders see planning as the key to success. Asked to state the essentials for effective organizational management, their reply is sure to include planning.

While supporting planning publicly, many leaders are skeptical privately. They may have participated in a state-of-the-art planning exercise, or they know someone who has, and they were left disappointed. Even when they intend to plan, nonprofit leaders are not always sure how to go about it. They are busy and, against the press of operations needing to be done now, put off planning.

Planning is not a panacea nor is it optional. Planning is, we agree, an essential part of organizational management. There is good planning and bad planning, but not planning is *not* an option for a nonprofit that wants to be around to greet the twenty-first century. The future, we are convinced, belongs to those who plan for it.

What Do We Mean by Planning?

Planning not only helps us to anticipate the future, it permits us, within limits, to *create* our future. In the absence of planning we are the victims of our fate. We take what we get. We are totally in a reactive mode. Through planning we can be proactive. We can have influence, not total control, over the events which come into our lives.

A plan is a framework for collective effort. It permits everyone in an organization to see his/her contribution in the context of the whole. A single musician can play by ear, but an orchestra needs music.

By planning we simulate the potential consequences of a given activity, both negative and positive. By planning we anticipate the likely outcome of an action, permitting adjustments which lessen the negative consequences and accentuate the positive consequences. Good planning is one of the most cost-effective activities an organization can undertake.

Planning is not making tomorrow's decisions today. The purpose of planning is not to decide what should be done in the future but to decide what should be done now to make desired things happen in an uncertain future.

A *plan* is by its very nature static. It is frozen in time. It cannot be otherwise. *Planning* is, by way of contrast, dynamic. It is an action verb. It lives. It reaches out and thrusts itself ever onward. This is what caused an experienced nonprofit leader to say, "The plan is nothing—but planning is everything."

Who Plans?

To whom is this important function assigned? Repeatedly organizations have attempted to make planning a discipline which stands on its own, to assign it to a special unit or a consultant, always with disappointing results. Planning is effective only when it is an integrated part of management. Planning apart from management leads to what is known as SPOTS

(Strategic Plans On Top Shelf). Management devoid of planning leads to irrelevance.

Planning is a part of every job description. The main difference is that the planning horizon gets shorter while the detail grows greater as the action moves down the organizational pyramid. For entry level workers planning may have to do with hours or days. Board and executive planning is, by way of contrast, concerned with years and even decades. It is comparably "broad brush." In one form or another, however, everyone plans, and the nature of those plans must be appropriate to the position each person occupies in the organization.

The board is responsible to assure that planning occurs and to establish the parameters within which planning takes place. Perhaps most important of all, the board demonstrates by word and deed that planning is an integral part of leading and managing an effective organization. Management is authorized to act strategically and is held accountable for doing so.

How to Plan

The planning format must be appropriate to the organization to which it belongs. Many boards and staffs have been disappointed in their planning efforts because they used borrowed or inappropriate models. A one-size-fits-all mentality leads to disappointing results.

Unfortunately, the field of *nonprofit* planning is not well developed. Many books do not even include planning in their indexes. Consequently, many nonprofits borrow their planning methods from the corporate world and may feel like David in Goliath's armor.

Our suggested planning outline is summarized in the Generic Planning Model (see Figure 5). It views planning from a *board* perspective since that is the focus of this book. It assumes a Stage V organization, so that organ-

FIGURE 5

Generic Planning Model (from a board perspective)

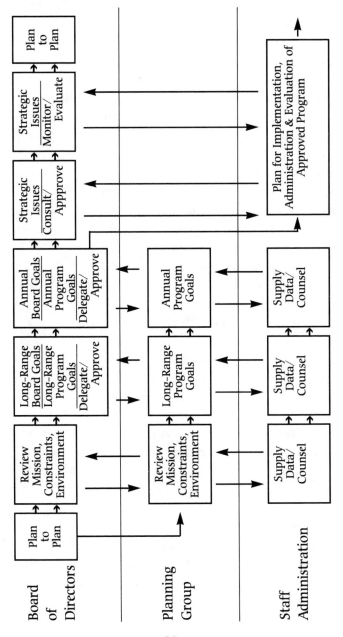

izations which are not at that stage need to make adaptations accordingly.

The Plan to Plan: The first step in a formal planning process is for the board to draw up a "plan to plan." In so doing, the *board* is accepting responsibility for the process. Through planning, a board is being proactive; it is leading. Boards that do not take an active role in the planning process are placed into a reactive mode. A board can and must delegate some planning functions to the administration, but the responsibility for initiating a strategic organizational plan resides with the board. The process begins with answering the following questions:

1. **To whom is the task of designing the plan assigned?** We suggest a committee of from three to seven members, depending on the size and complexity of the organization. It may include both board and staff. All those who are expected to participate in the plan should be represented on the committee. Persons who are well acquainted with the organization's history and persons who are known to be innovators should be included.

2. **What is the committee to do?** The assignment should be in written form and should state the expected end result. If the assignment has limitations, they should be stated in the memo of assignment.

3. **What documents and information does the committee need to complete its assignment?** This should include major reports, annual program plans and budgets, a statement of organizational purpose, mission, and vision. Most of all, it should include the last strategic planning report.

4. **How should the committee organize itself?** The board normally asks the CEO to serve as the committee chair. Additionally, the committee may have a secretary or recorder. In a large organization it is wise to assign a

staff person to help with calling meetings, gathering materials, distributing reports, etc.

5. **When is the committee expected to render its final report, and are there predetermined checkpoints in the process?** Specific dates should be agreed upon and recorded in memo form.

Planning Foundations: The planning process begins with a "situation audit" which identifies the elements, both internal and external, which will impact the plan. Some of these elements are predetermined and cannot be altered, but should still be recognized. Other elements need to be challenged critically and updated. We suggest three categories of planning foundations:

1. **Purpose/Mission/Vision.** The focus of planning is on the Ends an organization wants to achieve. Have the purpose, mission, and vision been stated with sufficient clarity? The three are similar in meaning, but they should not be thought of as synonymous.

Purpose states the organization's reason for existence. It states the anticipated *results*.

Mission defines the *method* which will be used in carrying out the organization's purpose. It answers the questions organizational leaders should be asking continually: "What is your business—what *should* it be?"

Vision describes an organization's preferred *future* state. What do its leaders want it to *become*? For what do they want it to be remembered?

In all three areas it is important to remember the universal rule of planning—no organization will ever be greater than the vision that drives it.

The drafters of purpose/mission/vision statements should work for brevity. A paragraph of eight or ten lines is ideal for a public statement. It is good to have a more detailed statement for internal board use, in order to elaborate on the philosophy which undergirds the public statement. One highly successful organization we know states its mission on a credit-card-sized card and gives one to each employee. If the employee can produce the card when asked to do so by the president in a chance meeting, she/he is rewarded with a five dollar bill.

The purpose/mission/vision statement is the single most important statement a board adopts because it defines why the organization exists. It is the heart from which everything else emanates. In navigational terms, it is the North Star.

2. **Constraints/Assumptions.** Constraints may be self-imposed; for example, "Our business is day care." Constraints may also be imposed by the legal charter. Legal constraints should be recognized even if they cannot be altered, but self-imposed constraints can and should be challenged; for example, *why* do we limit our activities to day care or to certain prescribed geographical areas or types of service?

Assumptions help to establish the parameters for planning. It is useful, even necessary, to state explicitly what the planners assume about the availability of funds and staff or the anticipated effect of pending legislation. Sound plans are created from correct assumptions. When plans are based on incorrect assumptions, they cannot be other than faulty. And when the assumptions change on which a plan is based, the plans must be adjusted accordingly.

The experience of hoteliers in the early 1950s illustrates the importance of correct assumptions. They had every reason to assume that the logical place for new facilities was in the downtown districts. That is where the action was. Only by scanning the horizon were they able to see the coming of air travel and the Federal Highways Act which would keep traffic on cities' outskirts. The prevailing assumptions were wrong, leading to costly errors from which some were unable to recover.

3. **Reading the environment.** It is useful in planning to distinguish between the internal and the external environments.

Internal: What do we do well? What are our strengths and weaknesses? Our vulnerabilities? It is useful to identify an organization's core activities and evaluate their future viability. What is the average age of your work force? Of your key people? Are you state-of-the-art or is technology passing you by? Is your facility adequate? Are your employees being trained?

Careful attention should be given to what is happening on the periphery. What are the new opportunities that are waiting for their turn under the sun? Organizational leaders should remember that the Swiss had their first turn at the revolutionary digital watch, but they turned it down because of their single-minded commitment to the conventional watch (another illustration of faulty assumptions).

External: What opportunities and threats face us? One of the most limiting traits of an organizational leader is to assume the future will be like the past. It will not be! We do not see change coming if we are not looking for it.

What economic, political, sociological, or technological changes are on the horizon? What is our competition doing? Very few changes make their appearances out of nowhere. The precursors are there, but we choose to ignore them until the urgency is great. Then it is often too late. In this fast paced world, an activity or a technology which has been in place for ten years is suspect. It may still have some useful life remaining, but it should be evaluated regularly and critically.

The board is responsible to lay the planning foundation by carefully probing and analyzing what is happening in these three areas. In our Planning Model, the planning group begins by reviewing what the board has concluded in these critical areas. In this process the board and the planning group should be interacting with each other, because the end result is foundational and must be owned by both groups.

From Board to Program Planning

This is the stage at which the planning process is divided into two parts. Having laid the foundation, the board delegates *program* planning to the planning group while it concentrates on its board *governance* planning. The board agrees to a calendar of activities. It identifies the major issues it wants to address. It decides what committees will be needed and defines their duties and responsibilities. It decides how often it wants to meet and when and where. It identifies its future membership needs. And it remembers to monitor and evaluate the program it approved the preceding year.

The planning group identifies both long-range and annual program goals. Long-range goals, generally thought of as being from three to five years in length, are not intended to be operational. Their main function is to establish the context for annual planning which *is* operational. Annual planning apart from the longer view often ends up being too shortsighted.

Long-range plans are more general than annual goals. Attempts to project five-year goals which are as specific and detailed as annual plans are not only counterproductive, they are frustrating. A development organization, for example, may identify continents and countries for future concentration. The naming of specific villages is best left for the annual plan.

Drawing from the purpose/mission/vision statement which defines *what* will be done, the long-range planning process focuses more on where, how, and how much. It seeks to identify what resources will be required and suggests what needs to be done to insure their availability.

A very useful line of long-range planning inquiry is what activities or services should be increased or decreased? Which should be introduced and which should be phased out?

The process of setting goals involves establishing priorities. Since resources are finite and organizations can't do everything, the process of goal-setting also determines what an organization will *not* do. This is difficult, and it is often painful, but it is necessary. Peter Drucker says it forcefully: "You must think through priorities. That's easy to say, but to act on it is very hard because doing so always involves abandoning things that look attractive, or giving up programs that people both inside and outside the organization are strongly encouraging. But if you don't concentrate your institution's resources, you are not going to get results. This may be the ultimate test of leadership: the ability to think through the priority decision and to make it stick."

Once the broad outlines have been identified, it is useful to set some specific targets so that all elements in the program can be adjusted accordingly. The addition of fifty hospital beds, for example, has serious and immediate implications for the physical plant, staffing, and cash flow. At this stage, the process does not need to go into architectural detail; indeed it should not. But identifying the broad goal permits the whole organization to anticipate and adjust its planning accordingly.

Establishing the *correct* target is both important and difficult. The electric utility industry in the 1980s seriously overestimated the nation's power needs, with

89

the result that it finds itself with much under-utilized capacity. Under-estimation can have equally unfortunate consequences. Computer models can help with this kind of projection, but finally these decisions are based on human judgment.

The planning group is expected to recommend its completed work to the board for adoption. Before the board gives its final approval, it should review the report thoroughly, even critically. Few things are of greater importance. Once officially adopted, the plan becomes the basis by which the organization's mission is accomplished.

Implementation Is Delegated

The planning group has completed its assignment. It should be thanked and dissolved. The board now delegates the approved plan to the administration for implementation. The board should incorporate several elements in the delegation process:

1. **Assure the administration of its confidence and support.** This is an opportunity to reinforce the partnership relationship which needs to exist between the board and the administration.

2. **Insure that the resources are available for plan implementation.** Few things are so demoralizing and counterproductive as to draw up ambitious plans and not be able to put them into action.

3. **Clarify the policies (and limitations) which are expected to guide program implementation.** Do they give the administration the guidance they need to meet board expectations?

4. **Provide for monitoring and evaluation. Effective delegation involves both letting go and keeping in touch.** Boards who do not let go of administrative detail demoralize staff and overburden themselves, often to the neglect of their governance

function. Boards who do not stay in touch are irrelevant to what is or is not happening and abdicate their responsibility. An appropriate middle position must be found.

The board is responsible to establish key performance indicators for major areas of activity. For example, in an effort to be an effective employer who seeks to foster personal growth, the board may adopt an objective that staff turnover should not exceed 10 percent per annum. Such a specific guideline helps the staff to know what is expected and by what standards its performance will be evaluated. It gives the board the confidence that it is doing its job.

An organization that is willing to learn puts considerable emphasis on evaluation. It strives continually to learn from its negative and positive experiences. The results of this ongoing evaluation are continually channeled back into and influence the administration and planning process.

The board is able to evaluate an organization's workings in distinctly different ways than the administration can. Distance is often seen as a disadvantage, but it can also be an advantage in that it increases perspective. Being removed can increase objectivity. It can improve overall comprehension.

The purpose of evaluation, it should be recognized, is not to expose deficiencies. Instead, it is to determine that the mission and goals of the organization are being achieved in the most efficient and effective way possible.

"Plan to Plan II"

As the year comes to a close, the planning process comes full circle. A new effort begins to once again review the five-year plan, adding the new year and dropping the previous fifth year. The process begins with the board evaluating the year's performance against the plan which had been approved the previous year. It reviews its three-point Planning Foundations. It looks at its long-range goals and annual goals and makes a new projection. It makes a plan for its own board governance work and evaluates the procedures and policies by which the program implementation is delegated to the administration. An effective board always looks both back and ahead, deciding what it wants to do and how to go about doing it.

The tendency is for things which are done repeatedly to erode into meaningless routine. One antidote for this deadly temptation is to mandate a zero-based planning process every fifth year. Whereas routine planning proceeds from the base line, zero-based planning, as the term implies, is a new beginning.

Effective directors are always looking for ways to improve the performance of the organization which they have been elected to lead. To actively involve the directors in the ongoing planning process is one of the best ways to fulfill this responsibility.

Planning is a vital part of managing. Planning has been viewed as a systematic approach to steering an enterprise through the uncertain waters of a rapidly changing environment to accomplish mission. Why then does Tom Peters, the modern day management guru say, "The odds of success increase to the extent to which we let go of our master plan"?

He is not saying, do not plan. He is also not advocating taking the plan lightly. What he is saying is do not elevate your plan to holy writ. Do not hold it too rigidly. Do not freeze things in place at the very time that change is accelerating all around you. Do not assume that the plan will replace on-the-spot decision-making. To paraphrase an old proverb, plan your work, work your plan—and be prepared to amend your plan to take new needs and opportunities into consideration.

12.

CONFLICT:
Inevitable, and Not Necessarily Bad

> *"Conflict is necessary and indispensable. There is no conflict only when no new decisions are made or no implementation of new decisions is necessary, which means death...Conflict is either destructive or constructive. It is never benign. It is constructive when it is functional; it is destructive when it is not channeled...What turns conflict into a destructive force is the lack of respect."*
> —Ichak Adizes in *Corporate Life Cycles*

Conflict is the inevitable result of human interaction. Wherever two or three are gathered, there will be differences which may lead to conflict.

Some useful parallels can be drawn between conflict and fire. Fire is one of life's essentials. We need it to cook, to keep warm, to cleanse, and to smelt. But when fire rages out of control it becomes unfriendly and even deadly.

Conflict can, in the same way, serve a useful purpose. It is evidence of life, that people care, that they are sufficiently committed to something to be in conflict over it. Conflict is evidence that there is more than one way of doing something.

But like fire, conflict can become destructive. It can distract or even destroy an organization. In the heat of the United States' biggest civil conflict Abe Lincoln said, "A house divided against itself cannot stand." The challenge facing leaders everywhere is to respond to conflict in such a way as to produce a positive outcome.

It is useful to understand the conflict behavioral styles which play themselves out in boardrooms.

Conflict Behavioral Styles

1. **Competing:** Directors who are competitive are intent upon winning. They set things up so that they win or get their way, and anyone who opposes them loses. They ignore, conceal, or diminish information which does not support their predetermined conclusion. They are individualistic and decisive and thrive especially in crisis situations. Their style requires others to submit rather than to think creatively and independently.

2. **Accommodating:** Directors who are accommodating are quick to support what appears to be the prevailing point of view. They hesitate to oppose or seek other solutions. They dislike conflict intensely and are eager to arrive at a consensus. They want to be well liked by everyone.

3. **Avoiding:** Directors who are avoiding are clearly uncomfortable with any differing point of view. Because their first concern is to stay out of the crossfire of any dispute, they contribute little to finding the best solution. When the discussion heats up, they shut down.

4. **Compromising:** Directors who are compromising find consensus by combining those parts of a discussion on which there is agreement, in ways which are acceptable to the disputing parties. The art of compromise is part of the democratic process, and it has its place. Its limitation is that instead of working toward the best solution, it pulls

the discussion toward the lowest common denominator. A compromised solution is often shallow and temporary.

5. **Collaborating:** Directors who are collaborating are first interested in identifying a variety of promising approaches to the subject at hand. They invite debate and welcome all alternatives which strengthen the consensus which is emerging. Their interest is not so much in *who* wins and *who* loses, but in arriving at the best solution. The collaborative process takes longer, but the results are usually better and more enduring.

The first four behaviors are driven by self-interest. How can I win? How can I be liked? How can I avoid being embarrassed? Maybe I can be the hero by brokering a compromise. By way of contrast, collaborating directors are less self-interested and are first concerned with arriving at a conclusion which will best serve the cause.

The challenge of a board, and particularly its chair, is to create a trusting atmosphere where members feel sufficiently secure to express a differing or untested, but potentially promising, point of view. The focus should be on the issues, keeping turf and ego considerations out of it as much as humanly possible. Some directors find this easier than others, but it is the goal towards which effective directors aspire.

Destructive Conflict Threatens Nevertheless

What should a board do when differences have gone beyond the bounds of constructive dialogue, and they are faced with the foreboding prospect of destructive conflict, including the threat of disintegration? There are many different kinds of conflict, and conflicts go through different stages, but some general principles may be useful:

Don't overreact. Some organizations are so idealistic that they view the mere threat of trouble as the sky falling

in on them. Nonprofit organizations are especially prone
to overreact when there is the threat of adverse publicity
which may interfere with fund raising. Overreaction
usually exacerbates the problem.

Organizations are remarkably tough. They can survive
more adversity than is commonly recognized. Like ball
players who are required to play through a slump,
organizations need to keep functioning even when
calamity threatens.

Own the problem—don't ignore it. This is your
problem. It needs to be dealt with. Don't wish it away.
Don't attempt to suppress it. However much you may
regret it and however disruptive it may seem, view it as
an opportunity to correct a weakness which has surfaced.

Fix it—yourself. Don't turn immediately to the
outside. Remember that consultants don't make decisions
for you—they help you to identify the options and their
predicted consequences. Adversity is a time when leaders
prove their mettle—and earn their nonprofit salary! More
than ever, in a time of difficulty leaders must accept
responsibility and exercise leadership. Failure to do so
results in a vacuum which leads to rapid and unnecessary
deterioration. Facts become confused with speculation
and negative leadership may assert itself. In this situation
leaders must do two things simultaneously.

First, they must have a thorough and accurate
understanding of the situation. What is going on here?
What is the problem? The real problem is often disguised
by what turn out to be decoys. Leaders must maintain
open minds and resolutely refuse to be pushed into action
until they know the essential facts.

Second, while never attempting to suppress emotions,
leaders manage the crisis in such a way that reason
prevails over emotion. They do this best by
demonstrating that leadership is functioning, by

communicating openly, and by sharing the facts as they become available.

Once they know the facts, and before they make binding decisions, the board should consider its full range of options. It should not rush into a decision prematurely, but neither should it dally. It most assuredly should not procrastinate and shrink from a hard decision. It needs to shape a well developed proposal.

Seek outside help. Even as the doctor who treats himself has a fool for a patient, so there are situations where an organization must turn to the outside for help. Doing so may be a sign of strength. One such time may be when the leaders themselves are involved in the conflict, and they often are. Some may lament, "Isn't this a sorry state of affairs we have fallen into?" Not necessarily. The sorry state may follow if help is not found.

Mediation is a form of conflict resolution being used increasingly in nonprofit and church settings. It is a process in which a trained and objective third party helps those in conflict find a mutually agreeable solution. The field of conflict resolution has grown to include mediation to resolve insurance claims, business disputes, and neighborhood conflicts. It also includes intra-group and organizational consulting in which a third party assists groups working through difficult situations. There are a wide variety of organizations and individuals who offer mediation and consulting services for individuals or groups in conflict. Many of these offer training in conflict resolution as well.

Our strong inclination is to avoid litigation, but not necessarily at all costs. It, too, is a form of conflict resolution, albeit a drastic and a costly one. For all its limitations, litigation is to be preferred over protracted conflict.

We conclude by recalling a board meeting in a church setting where sharp differences had been expressed. Two men who were each deeply committed to the cause and independent in their thinking held on to what appeared to be irreconcilable differences. The time for adjournment came before agreement had been reached. One of the disputants was asked to offer a closing prayer. After a brief pause, he rose to the occasion with a beautiful, conciliatory prayer. I don't remember the full text of it, but it included the line, "Thank you for those who differ with us. They help us in ways that those who always agree with us never do."

13.

LEGAL DIMENSIONS:
The Risks Involved in Doing Good

> *"No obstacle [to volunteer service] is more chilling than
> the fear of personal liability and the high cost of
> insurance to protect against liability."*
> —George Bush

Board service has long been seen as a duty and an honor,
and so it is. It is one way in which persons who have
achieved a level of success are able to make their talents
available to the wider community. The value of services
given in this way is inestimable.

There has been, in recent years, an erosion of charitable
immunity. Directors serve under the possibility of
personal liability. As society has become more litigious,
the exposure has extended from the for-profit to the
nonprofit sector. Today, both are held to the same
standard of conduct.

Each person is expected to be responsible and to act in
a reasonable manner which does not harm others. When
a person accepts service on a board, he or she assumes the
responsibility for directing and managing the affairs of an
organization and is expected to act in a certain way. Thus,
each director and officer should prepare to assume some

level of personal risk which unavoidably accompanies such service.

Directors and officers (D&O) should not be paranoid about this liability, but neither should they be naive about it. Directors obviously have self-interest in maintaining their personal assets. They are also responsible to direct as many organizational resources (financial, human, etc.) as possible toward accomplishing the mission and goals of the organization, rather than paying indemnity or excessive D&O insurance premiums. This is vital to good stewardship.

Wrongful Acts as Sources of Liability

Liability generally occurs when there is an injury or harm caused by a wrongful act. The party responsible for causing the injury is made to pay the costs.

D&O liability has to do with wrongful acts committed by directors and officers. The term "wrongful acts" is defined technically as "any negligent act, error, commission, breach of duty, misstatement, misleading statement, or other act done or willfully attempted by the directors or officers acting in their capacities as such." Thus, a director or officer must have acted or failed to act according to some standard of care which is expected of directors and officers.

Thus, wrongful acts need not be willful wrongdoing. They may, in fact, be ever so innocent or, at times, may even seem unavoidable. The following illustrations depict the types of circumstances which can confront nonprofit organizations:

Grievance: A board moves to terminate an employee for what appears to be "just cause." Later the fired employee contends that her civil rights were violated and her professional career damaged. Suit is brought and the board and organization are made to defend themselves.

Moral Impropriety: An employee is found to be engaging in sexual misconduct. A parent of one of the victims brings suit, contending that serious psychological damage has been done to his child. In the investigation, it is discovered that the charged employee has a record of similar offenses, but the pre-employment screening procedure had not been sufficiently thorough to discover it. The organization is made to defend itself against the charge of negligence.

Preventive Maintenance: A fire kills two elderly nursing home residents. In the investigation it is learned that a few months earlier a mechanical engineering firm evaluated the physical plant. The report which was submitted to the board warns that some equipment is unreliable and needs to be replaced. Carelessness is alleged.

These examples demonstrate that the board is responsible to monitor and manage the risks to which the organization and each director or officer is subject. The board, each director, officers, and CEO, therefore, should periodically engage in a process of: (1) identifying and analyzing risks, (2) selecting and implementing risk prevention programs, and (3) allocating the costs in the event that there is a loss. This should be done with the help of an attorney who can explain what legal risks the directors and officers and the organization face. Also, an attorney can assist in developing and implementing a risk-prevention program for the directors and officers. After identifying and assessing the risks and the likelihood of a loss, it is important to determine how the responsible party will pay the loss if one should occur.

Risk Identification and the Standard of Care

When identifying risks, it is important to determine how D&O liability might be imposed and who the injured party might be. Generally, D&O liability can be imposed upon a director when there is an injury caused by: (1) the breach of some standard of care, or (2) the violation of a statute or the application of strict liability. Having identified the cause of the injury, it is important to identify the injured party.

The Standards of Care, Loyalty, and Obedience

Traditionally, directors and officers have duties of care, loyalty, and obedience which are owed to the organization and each other. Although these specific duties may be expressed in different terms from state to state, directors and officers are expected to exercise their duties in good faith, in a manner which is reasonably believed to be in the best interests of the organization, and with the care exercised by an ordinarily prudent person.

The duty of care or diligence implies extending the care that a reasonably prudent person in a similar position would use under similar circumstances. Prior to making a business decision, directors or officers should inform themselves of all material information reasonably available to them. This can be demonstrated by taking the time necessary, on an ongoing basis, to understand the operations and finances of the organization.

The duty of loyalty is based upon acting in good faith and in the best interests of the organization. Thus, directors and officers are required to refrain from engaging in personal activities which may injure or take advantage of the organization. They are prohibited from using their positions of trust and confidence to further their private interests. This duty requires an undivided and unselfish loyalty to the organization and demands that there be no conflict between one's duty to the organization and self-interest.

The duty of obedience requires directors and officers to

perform their duties in accordance with applicable statutes and the terms of the organization's charter. Directors and officers may be liable if they authorize an act which is beyond the powers conferred upon a corporation by its charter or by applicable federal or state law. A breach of any of these duties will generally injure the organization or the fellow directors and officers. Thus, the organization and fellow directors and officers can bring suit against a director and officer.

Statutory or Strict Liability

Some statutes will hold a director liable for certain acts or omissions of the organization. Federal income tax law, the Employee Retirement Income Security Act (ERISA), and environmental laws contain provisions which can hold a director liable in certain cases.

Third Party Liability

A director or officer may be named in a lawsuit by the mere fact that he or she is a director or officer. These lawsuits are generally known as third party suits and involve personal injury or damage to property. In these suits, a third party (i.e., not a director, officer, or member of the organization, nor the state attorney general) is injured by either the organization or by an agent acting within the scope of his or her duties. The third party can seek to recover damages from the organization and, in doing so, may even name the directors individually in the lawsuit.

Generally, the corporation, and not the directors and officers, will be liable for these injuries. The organization's general liability and property insurance policies should cover these costs.

To add clarity to this subject and restore some aspects of charitable immunity, some states have enacted laws which provide volunteer directors and officers and volunteer workers with immunity. This immunity, however, is provided to a director, officer, or volunteer for acts which are not intentional, wanton, or grossly negligent. Despite this statutory immunity and regardless if the director, officer, or volunteer are ultimately liable, a person can still be named in a suit which requires defending oneself.

Risk Assessment

There are many techniques for assessing the risk associated with D&O liability. In determining which technique(s) to use, it is important to perform an assessment of the likelihood of a loss and the amount of the loss if it should occur (including the legal costs associated with a defense of a lawsuit).

1. **Avoidance.** Some risks of D&O liability can be eliminated entirely by not engaging in hazardous activity. A hospital board may refuse to authorize certain types of high risk treatment which avoids exposing the hospital and the board to the risk of liability. Liability, therefore, may be a factor in deciding if a new service should be initiated.

2. **Reduction.** The degree of risk can be materially reduced through loss control procedures. Some boards require each director and officer to identify on an annual basis significant and other interests which could pose conflicts of interest. The board would know ahead of time when there is a potential conflict of interest by one of its members.

Also, it is wise for a board to conduct an annual orientation for new and existing board members so that they are thoroughly knowledgeable about the activities of the organization and the board's responsibilities. Most boards require that their organizations' financial and other pertinent information be submitted to them on a regular basis and prior to each board meeting so that each director and officer can be prepared to discuss the issues. Adequate minutes of meetings which document the discussions and activities can reduce exposure.

3. **Separation.** A multifaceted nonprofit organization may create a separate corporation for one of its more hazardous activities, and thus insulate the host organization and its directors and officers from liability. It does not reduce the potential liability of the board of the separate corporation. Each board should use similar risk management techniques.

4. **Retention.** An organization may choose to be self-insured on at least some of its risk through the election of a deductible and through the limits of the insurance. This may take the form of creating a self-insurance fund which, as it grows, makes possible an increased deductible and lower limits. Note should be taken of the fact that self-insurance is not synonymous with "going bare." To the extent the organization is unable to meet its obligations through insurance or its resources, each director and officer may face potential liability and may be retaining some risks.

5. **Transfer.** The costs can be transferred by a contract. This is usually done through the purchase of insurance, but it can also take the form of indemnification which can be provided by law or by contract.

Indemnification for Directors and Officers

Many states have adopted legislation which permits nonprofit organizations to indemnify or reimburse directors and officers for amounts they may be called upon to pay to satisfy a judgment brought against them in their capacities as directors or officers or money spent on their legal defenses. Some states have permissive indemnification, which means the organization has some discretion and must decide to provide the indemnification through a provision in the articles of incorporation, bylaws, or resolution, or through a separate agreement with each director or officer. Other states have mandatory indemnification which provides that a director is entitled by law to indemnification when certain statutory conditions have been met. Also, if state law permits it, organizations should consider advancing defense costs.

The indemnification provision is useful, but, in and of itself, it is not adequate protection for directors and officers. First, it is limited in its application. Indemnification is improper if the directors or officers breach their duties as stated in this chapter. Personal liability for fines or punitive damages may not be indemnified because of the public interest in holding individuals responsible when they willfully violate established rules. Finally, the indemnification provision is only as good as the resources an organization has to make good on its agreement to reimburse.

The organization, therefore, should consider obtaining a directors and officers liability insurance policy, because the policy covers the wrongful acts of the directors and officers *and* the indemnification which an organization may be required to pay. This policy strengthens the indemnification provision in that it expands the resources an organization has available to it.

What You Are Buying When You Buy D&O Insurance

In addition to indemnification, directors and officers can also transfer the costs of liability through the purchase of insurance. Insurance policies have deductibles, exclusions, and limits which means that the transfer is partial. If the policy limits are reached, then the directors and officers or the organization (if indemnification is in effect) must cover the loss.

A D&O insurance policy generally contains two parts to its coverage: (1) the policy covers errors and omissions of the directors and officers; and (2) the policy covers amounts the organization is obligated to pay directors and officers because of indemnification. D&O liability insurance does not cover liability for personal injuries or property damage which are generally third party actions and covered under a general liability policy.

The insuring agreement protects an organization with respect to its indemnification and the directors and officers with respect to "loss" arising from claims lodged against them by reason of a "wrongful act." "Loss" is generally defined as including costs, charges, and expenses incurred in the defense of actions, suits, or proceedings. The usual coverage is fairly broad, but there are a number of standard exclusions which normally include: (1) libel and slander; (2) benefits obtained through personal gain; (3) unlawful distributions; and (4) dishonesty. Bodily injury, property damage claims, pollution claims, and intra-board suits are also common exclusions. Some of these claims would be a part of the general liability or property insurance policies.

Careful attention should be given to whether the policy is written on an occurrence or a claims-made basis. With occurrence coverage, an incident is covered if it occurs within the policy period. Coverage under a claims-made policy depends on the claim being filed during the policy period. If a claim is not filed until a specified later date, the claim may not be honored.

It is important to establish that the policy being bought includes a provision for defense. First, defense is where the major expenses occur. A survey the Wyatt Company took in 1988 revealed that 60% of all claims were closed without payment to the claimant. The same study revealed that the average time lag from claim to disposition was 5.25 years. A defense, even against what may appear to be a frivolous charge, can be very expensive. Second, the value of insurance is not only in the ability to pay, but also in the experience and expertise an insurance company has to put together in a good defense. Some organizations feel that defense is one of the most important provisions within an insurance policy.

Prevention by the Organization

It is important to implement a risk prevention program in conjunction with the insurance purchased. This program demonstrates to donors and volunteers that an organization is concerned about good stewardship. In addition, the better the loss record (i.e., the fewer the losses), the less likely that insurance premiums will increase substantially.

The likelihood of wrongdoing by directors and officers can be reduced by the adoption of good board meeting procedures. Meetings should be held regularly and in a businesslike atmosphere. Ample time should be allowed to deal with complex issues. The agenda and background papers should be distributed well in advance of the meetings. Minutes should not only record actions, but they should also summarize the major considerations which went into decisions. The results of all votes taken should be recorded, along with the names of directors who voted against the action. In a particularly crucial situation, it may be in order to ask legal counsel to review the minutes before they are approved.

Written procedures and instructions on a variety of sensitive administrative subjects, i.e., grievance procedures, sexual misconduct, etc., can reduce wrongdoing and strengthen the defense if legal action is brought. The key to any risk prevention program is to follow through with the implementation of the policies and procedures which reduce the risk of liability. Additionally, it is vital to document continued adherence to the program in the minutes and corporate records.

Prevention by Individual Directors and Officers

There are things which individual directors and officers can do to enhance their performance and, at the same time, reduce the likelihood of wrongdoing:

1. Directors should attend all board and pertinent committee meetings.

2. Directors should demonstrate good faith; they must meet the prudency test.

3. Newly elected/appointed directors and officers should acquaint themselves with the bylaws, the mission statement, employment manuals, and written statements of policy and procedure. It is also wise for them to read the minutes of the board meetings held in the previous year or two.

4. Each director should identify conflicts of interest when such is known to exist and should decline to participate in a decision where conflict of interest can be alleged.

5. If the organization does not have directors' and officers' liability insurance, it may be possible for individual directors to have limited coverage endorsed onto their homeowners policies.

6. Any director casting a negative vote on a resolution which is adopted should be so recorded in the minutes.

7. Directors and officers who are not comfortable with procedures and actions should consider resigning if they are unable to gather adequate support for changes which they believe are necessary.

Conclusion

D&O insurance extends to the liability of the directors and officers in performance of their duties (of care, loyalty, and obedience). It also covers an organization for whatever it pays out pursuant to indemnification. The insurance does not otherwise cover an organization's liabilities which are subject to a commercial general liability policy. One of the benefits of D&O insurance is that legal defense costs are covered. Thus, if there is a possibility that a director or officer will be sued, D&O insurance helps to cover the legal costs and expenses incurred.

Each organization should be concerned with stewardship of resources. An organization should avoid subjecting any person to an unnecessary risk of loss. This can be done with a good risk prevention program and insurance, if appropriate.

Directors and officers should not be paranoid, but neither should they be naive. They should, if they believe in the cause they have been elected to represent, be prepared to assume some level of risk which unavoidably accompanies their service.

For the information contained in this chapter, we gratefully acknowledge the collaboration of Peter Beard who served as the corporate attorney for Habit for Humanity until 1993.

14.

RENEWAL:
Preventing a Premature Death

> *"In an ever-renewing society, what matures is a system or a framework within which continuous innovation, renewal, and re-birth can occur."*
> —John W. Gardner

Like humans, organizations have a limited life span. It is startling to realize that many organizations do not survive their founder by more than 10 years. Organizations, to draw on the biblical metaphor, spring up, they flourish for a time, then they linger and die. If organizations were given a formal burial like people, the graveyard would be enormous. The message of this chapter is that organizations can be renewed. Their useful life can be extended.

Remarkable recuperative powers are part of creation. My wife and I (Edgar) were living in Europe when CIBA-GEIGY accidentally spilled large quantities of poisonous chemicals into the Rhine River. Once the extent of the damage had been assessed, many believed that the Rhine was destined to be a dead body, good only for navigational purposes. Anyone who has lived on the banks of this beautiful, historic river knows how depressing that thought was. Newspapers daily traced the movement of the spill as it wove its way from Switzerland, through Germany and Holland, and finally out to the North Sea. On a visit four years later, we were pleased to learn that aquatic life was returning much sooner than had been thought possible. Renewal is an integral part of creation.

What is true of the physical world applies also to the world of sociology. Organizations wind down, and, if their mission is lost, they disappear. The United States of America, for all its problems, serves as a good illustration of a renewable system. Established more than 200 years ago, it has been racked by scandals of every kind. It seems always to be in the shadow of a looming crisis. But it has survived because its founders, in all their wisdom and after years of vigorous debate, put in place a system which is capable of self-correction. Contrast it, for example, with the Soviet Union which very quickly reached an extreme state of rigidity and which, after a mere 70 years, has disintegrated.

When asked, "What is the one most difficult thing that you personally need to work on?" Max DePree, chairman of the Herman Miller Company said, "The interception of entropy." Unless deliberate care is given and action is taken, organizations run out of steam.

Practical Suggestions for Organizational Renewal

Review the Mission. Is it relevant? Is it focused? Is it bold? Most probing of all, do you believe in it?

The story is told of people living along a rocky coast in Nova Scotia where shipwrecks were a common occurrence. After a particularly sad tragedy, they mounted a campaign to build a lighthouse. The cause was urgent and people gave generously. Soon the lighthouse was in operation. Volunteers were recruited to staff it.

When it became hard to recruit volunteers, staff was employed. Modern equipment was purchased. One year more money was collected than was needed for operations, so it was decided to equip the staff lounge so that off-duty workers could be more comfortable.

With the passage of time, coastal traffic decreased and ships were equipped with radar. The purpose for which the organization had been called into being had disappeared, but funds were available and old-timers had an emotional commitment to the cause. Leaders had failed to identify a new need, and thus the lighthouse effort continued for a time, even though no function was being served.

Organizations faced with low morale and disappointing fund drives should not be quick to conclude that the solution resides in a multicolor brochure or a more vigorous fund-drive chair. The deeper problem may be that the program has lost its relevance and urgency.

Review the People. "Organizations," observes John W. Gardner, "go to seed when the people in them go to seed. And they awaken when the people awaken. The renewal of organizations and societies begins with people." This may be either through enlisting new people or by the renewal of people already in the system. It must take place continuously at all levels of the organization, from entry level positions to career personnel to the board of directors.

New people bring new energy and new perspectives. They ask questions which persons who have been in the system no longer ask. They decide for themselves if the answers being given are adequate. A system is in trouble when it can no longer attract a stream of new talent.

Renewal happens when people have a future orientation, when they are driven by something they want to accomplish, when they care. Leaders can achieve renewal only if they believe in the possibility of it.

Review Your Plan. Does it commit you to specific goals? Are the identified goals challenging and are they achievable? Does your plan contain benchmarks against which to measure your progress or lack of it? Planning is one of the best ways a board has to exercise leadership and renewal.

Welcome Change. As organizations mature and achieve a measure of success, their tendency is to conserve, to live on the laurels of their past accomplishments. Like a basketball team with a history of success, organizations who are proud of their past may no longer dive for the loose ball. They hesitate to risk change. It is stated beautifully by Niccoló Machiavelli: " There is nothing more difficult to attempt, more perilous to conduct, or more uncertain in its success, than to take the lead in the introduction of a new order of things. Because the innovator has for enemies all those who have done well under the old conditions, and only lukewarm defenders in those who might do well under the new."

Learn from Others. There is so much we can learn from others, and they are surprisingly willing to share it, if asked. Plan a retreat with a well chosen retreat person. Attend association meetings. Read relevant books and articles. Engage a consultant.

 Learn from Your Mistakes—and avoid repeating them. Few things are more demoralizing than failure and the loss of confidence which comes with repeating mistakes.

Denounce the Status Quo. "Bureaucracies," says Laurence Peter of Peter Principle fame, "defend the status quo long past the time when the quo has lost its status."

Evaluate Your Corporate Culture. Does a positive spirit of teamwork prevail? Is there a commitment to excellence? Are relationships built on trust and mutual respect? Is it permissible to risk a new idea? Is the mission owned by all who are expected to contribute to it?

Organizations, like people, have their good times and their bad times. One experienced leader made the sage observation to his successor, "Things are usually not as good as they appear when they are up nor as bad as they appear when they are down."

When an organization is down, the temptation is to draw in, to retreat to a defensive position. Leaders, with the best of intentions, emphasize control and caution when vision and faith are most needed. The last act of an organization, it has been observed, is to enlarge the rule book. Its focus is on doing things right when it should be on doing the right things.

DePree reminds us that "We cannot become what we need to be by remaining what we are." The renewing person, as well as the renewing organization, must be mature enough to be self-critical and admit, "We can do better." They must care enough to risk change.

15.

LEAVING RIGHT:
Signing Off

> *"For everything there is a season—a time to engage and a time to disengage."*
>
> —A paraphrase from the
> Old Testament book, Ecclesiastes

Leaving can be a satisfying experience. A director has served well, and now the time has come to move on, making room for someone else to serve. It is a smooth and natural passage from something completed to something waiting. It is a time of reflection and thanksgiving. It is a cherished moment for both the retiring officeholder and those who remain to continue the work.

Leaving can also be a difficult time. Deep and meaningful relationships are not easily severed. Occasionally, persons leave boards feeling hurt and alienated from the very things they have worked so hard to build.

This should not be. This does not need to be. Organizations and their boards should give as much thought and planning to termination as they do to recruitment and orientation.

Expectations

In some organizations, a pattern exists whereby directors assume that unless they disgrace themselves, election is for as long as they want to serve. In an earlier generation those offices were sometimes conferred on directors' sons. It is not easy for a board to break this dynamic without hurting persons' feelings. Our advice to boards who find themselves in this situation is to be clear, be firm, be patient, and above all, be loving. To paraphrase the Golden Rule, "Do unto retiring directors as you will want done unto you when the time comes." Leaving right involves as much thought and planning as installation. Organizations can act to make leaving easier and more positive.

1.   Help directors to have realistic expectations, including the idea of a positive termination. Board service should be thought of as a task and privilege which rotates. The adoption of term and/or age limits, as advocated in Chapter 2, guides directors as they subconsciously formulate their expectations.   Mennonite Indemnity, a Mennonite church insurance service, has a covenant of board service in which directors pledge that when the time comes they intend to "step aside graciously and with goodwill to their successors and the cause."

2.   Directors (and employees) should get frequent recognition for their contributions; such affirmation should not all be saved for retirement parties. The process of re-nomination to another term should be used as an opportunity to recognize what has been accomplished and to call for a new commitment. These moments can be handled in ways which reinforce the in (make your contribution)-and-out rhythm of board service.

3. There are special situations which call for flexibility. Even as directors are called upon to adjust their expectations when a new policy on board tenure is

adopted, so boards must be flexible in how their ground rules are applied. When a board, for example, adopts a service maximum, directors affected by this change deserve some special consideration. Some boards in this situation elect a director to a shorter term. Sometimes an extra year or two can be the difference between hurt or good feelings.

4. Ease the transition by providing for continued participation. A founding director, or someone who has served with distinction, may be given emeritus status. Someone with a unique gift or experience may be retained for a time as a consultant. Habitat for Humanity has a practice of electing former directors to the Board of Advisors and providing them with board meeting minutes for one year after their retirement. Most boards have a provision which permits directors to be brought back on the board after a year of leave.

Timing

Leaving right has a lot to do with timing. A director has found board service to be deeply satisfying and feels that she or he still has something unique to contribute. While many directors recall how some of their predecessors overstayed and vow not to do the same, privately they may entertain thoughts of indispensability. At least they may have grave doubts about the ability of young directors to uphold the proud tradition they have established and maintained. They see themselves now in that stage of life when they have more time for this type of service.

It is at such a moment that some directors get locked into a "one more term" syndrome. They may reluctantly hint at retirement, only to be greeted by a polite, "Oh Jake, what would we do without you?" Jake makes a few disclaimers and after a brief pause says, "Okay, one more term." Later as the younger directors discuss it among themselves, one recalls that this was a repeat of what was said when Jake was up for reelection last time.

Directors who stay one term too long no longer enjoy the respect of their fellow directors. Although everyone is polite, they begin to hear the message—it's time to move on. Jake must admit to himself that there are more things that he doesn't understand and feel a part of. Once the dynamic has reached this stage, it is hard for a director to leave right.

To leave right, a director must leave at the right time. Sometimes this is not possible, but this should be the goal for both the director and the organization. But be forewarned—leaving right, even though it may be properly handled, is still not necessarily easy. We are reminded of a church leader who, upon losing a close election, said that turning the work over to his successor was more difficult than to have done it for seventeen years.

Though this book is addressed specifically to directors, the concern for a positive termination applies equally to employees. They, no less than directors, have invested themselves in the cause and deserve appropriate recognition.

The importance of leaving right was brought home to me (Edgar) when a Mennonite Central Committee (MCC) overseas relief worker had an emotional breakdown which required her to return home for treatment. She responded well, but we were taken aback when the doctor advised that she be permitted to return to her former place of assignment so that she could "leave right." Didn't the doctor know or care that this meant expensive travel to a distant country? We allowed ourselves to be convinced, however, and in retrospect I feel MCC did what was owed this young church worker.

There are some things an organization can and should do to ease the adjustment of a retiring director, although some responsibility also resides with the director.

Leaving is inevitable. Leaving right is the last thing we should want after having contributed ourselves to a cause.

EXHIBIT 1

Job Description
for Board Members

1. Constituents

Board members are responsible to understand, represent, and communicate with their constituents and stakeholders to the best of their abilities. Board members should try to represent the highest and largest interests of those they represent and, least of all, their own special interests.

2. Mission

Determine the mission, long-range goals, philosophies, and general policies of the organization, making certain the organization meets the needs it was established to meet or others assigned to it.

Ensure the continuity, vitality, and faithfulness of the organization to its charter and bylaws until such a time that the mission of the organization is no longer necessary or has changed. This duty includes periodically reviewing the bylaws and other documents that establish the legal status of the organization and revising them as necessary.

3. Products or Services

Assure that the products or services meet the requests of clients and are truly legitimate needs of human beings, that the products and services fulfill the mission of the organization and faithfully meet the standards of quality subscribed to by the organization.

4. Financial

Determine and maintain strong financial direction and procedures of the organization, assuring its financial soundness.

5. Management

Assure that the organization is well managed and fulfilling its mission, primarily by selecting, appraising, supporting, and giving counsel to the chief executive officer, and that the organization is maintaining sound personnel policies.

6. Self-Control of the Board Itself

Determine policies and procedures to ensure the board's own strength, growth, organization, procedures, and effective representation and communication with constituents.

EXHIBIT 2

Orientation of Board Members
A Checklist

Date of Orientation	Topic	Accountable Person
	1. Overview	**Board Chairperson**
_____	History, mission, values, goals of organization	
	2. Board Organization and Expectations of Board Members	**Board Chairperson**
_____	Job description for board members	
_____	Board meetings: time, place	
_____	Preparation: agenda, minutes	
_____	Committees: assignment	
_____	Annual board cycle: annual meeting, future plans	
_____	Planning cycle: policies, practices	
_____	Relation of board members and staff	
_____	Time expectations: meetings	
_____	Introduction to all other board members and their roles	
_____	Retreats	
_____	Recent annual evaluations of CEO	
_____	Financial commitments and reimbursements: meals, liability	
_____	Contributions, travel	
_____	Description of board responsibilities (read and understood)	
_____	Bylaws (read and understood)	
	3. Organization's Place in the Community	**Vice Chairperson**
_____	Industry, market	
_____	Competitors, collaborators	
_____	Reputation	

Date of Orientation	Topic	Accountable Person
	4. Financial Review	*Treasurer*
_____	Long-range financial plan	
_____	Fund raising	
_____	Balance sheet	
_____	Profit and loss: operations sheets	
_____	Budget procedures and current budget	
_____	Funding sources: problems, auditors	
	5. Description and Tour of Operations, Facilities	*CEO*
_____	Products, services	
_____	Clients	
_____	Methods of service distribution	
_____	Tour of facilities	
_____	Introduction to key or all staff	
_____	Organization chart	
	6. Committee Assignment	*Committee Chairperson*
_____	Purpose of committee	
_____	Task of members	
_____	Arrangements/Meetings: time, place,	
_____	Preparation of agenda, minutes	
_____	Individual assignment	
	7. Other	

I have completed this orientation and am sufficiently familiar with this organization to begin functioning as a board member with my assigned roles and tasks.

Signed_____Date _____

EXHIBIT 3

Job Description for Board Chairperson

I. Function

The principal functions of the board chairperson are to lead and to facilitate the work of the board of directors and its relationship to the CEO.

II. Relationships and Functions

A. To the board

1. Responsible to board. The chair is usually elected by the board and responsible to it for his/her work.
2. Leads board to develop long-term and annual goals and to achieve goals.
3. Convenes and presides at board meetings.
   a. Responsible to see that annual tasks are accomplished.
   b. Develops agenda and relevant materials to be circulated prior to meetings.
   c. Manages agenda and time in order to fulfill tasks in an efficient way.
   d. Assures minutes are completed and sent immediately after all meetings.
   e. Seeks full participation of all members.
   f. Leads board in making sound decisions in order to fulfill the mission and goals of organization.
4. Communicates actions of board as necessary to assure implementation.

B. To the vice chairperson

1. In his/her absence, the chair will delegate powers and tasks to the vice chair.
2. The vice chair should be informed frequently of the chair's work and concerns so that the vice chair can substitute for the chair with minimal loss and stress.
3. May assign key tasks to the vice chair, such as designating committee chairs.

C. **To the Chief Executive Officer**
1. The chair works closely with the CEO to define the CEO's responsibilities, goals, and extent of his/her authority in a written job description. The CEO is accountable for all his/her work to the board, communicated through the board chair. (This is apart from the staff report which the CEO makes to the whole board.)
2. The chair conveys and interprets the values, goals, plans, concerns, and actions of the board to the CEO whenever such clarification is needed.
3. The chair conducts at least monthly meetings with the CEO to keep abreast of important organizational issues (personnel, financial condition, progress on goals) and the personal needs of the executive (vacations, professional development, staff relationships, job satisfaction, intentions about continuing in the position).
4. The chair and CEO meet following the CEO's annual report to evaluate the CEO's work during the preceding year and to assist the CEO in the setting of personal, professional, and organizational goals for the next year.
5. The chair communicates annually with the board and then the CEO about the CEO's compensation.
6. The chair maintains a close relationship with the CEO, so that the board is assured that the CEO is fulfilling their expectations and so that the CEO has someone with whom he/she can discuss the working situation.

D. **To the public(s)**
1. The chair is the board's spokesperson to its various publics, the press, and other media if board expression is advisable. Board members should not speak individually on behalf of the board unless assigned to do so by the chair.
2. The chair and CEO should confer before meeting the publics and support each other in that process.
3. The chair may represent the organization at various functions in coordination with the CEO.

Exhibit 3

4. The chair in his/her daily activities endeavors to listen carefully to public opinion about the organization and seeks the goodwill of others toward the organization.

5. In general, the chair is to watch over the total life and development of the organization, so that it is meeting genuine human needs and fulfilling its mission.

EXHIBIT 4

Annual Calendar of Board Tasks

This is a suggested calendar of board tasks. A board may identify different tasks but should coordinate them with its own meeting schedule.

1. Review the mission, values, and philosophy of management of the organization.

   —Mid-year

2. Set goals for the organization, both annual and long-term.
   —2-6 months prior to beginning of Fiscal Year (FY)

3. Approve plans of action proposed by the CEO by which the organization will achieve the goals set by the board.
   —1-3 months prior to beginning of FY

4. Financial: approve budget(s)—capital and operating—contributions, etc. Review investments, policies, procedures, results, changes, and borrowings.
   —1-3 months prior to beginning of FY

5. Establish regular meeting procedure and schedule for board and committees to accomplish goals.

   —Mid-year

6. Organize the board in order to achieve the goals of board.
   A. Committees
   B. Task Forces
   C. Consultants
   D. New members
   —According to the schedule outlined by the board

7. Monitor the progress of the management and company toward its goals through reports from the CEO, board committees, financial reports, and key staff.
   —At each board meeting

Exhibit 4

8. Orientation for new board members:
   A. To each other
   B. To the task of being a board member
   C. To the organization
   D. To the key staff
   E. To the organization's goals, values, needs, problems, etc.
   —*Immediately after new members are appointed*

9. Identify the most urgent issues calling for board attention and make a plan for how they will be addressed.
   —*1-3 months prior to beginning of FY*

10. Plan and conduct continuing education of board.
    —*Early in the new year*

11. Identify and make provision to supply information useful to the related publics (stakeholders) and provide for appropriate interaction, including annual reports, new program materials, announcements, etc.
    —*Throughout the year*

12. Review and evaluate annual report of the CEO. (This report should include financial, operations, and personnel reports.)
    —*2-3 months after close of FY, when annual report is complete*

13. Self-evaluation of board performance.
    —*2-3 months after close of FY*

EXHIBIT 5

General Outline for
Board Committee Accountability

A board may appoint whatever committees it chooses, subject to its own bylaws. Each committee should be given a written assignment, following or adapted from this general outline:

1. Name of committee
2. Committee membership
3. Staff liaison
4. Purpose
5. Duties and responsibilities
6. Reporting procedures/schedule
7. Committee budget
8. Projected schedule of meetings

Additional considerations:

1. The purpose (#4) of the board committee is to help the board (not the administration) do its work. Board committees study specific issues as assigned to them by the board (not the CEO), identify options, and draw up recommendations for board action. They do pre-board—not sub-board—work. It is important to recognize that the only authority a committee has is that which is assigned to it by the board.

2. The duties and responsibilities (#5) of board committees are assigned by the board annually in a manner so that the whole board and senior staff know what issues are being addressed. Individual committees should identify the specific issues they plan to address, but those suggestions are subject to board approval and should likewise be shared with the entire board and senior staff.

Exhibit 5

3. Reporting (#6). Items that a committee brings that require action should be presented in written form. This is sometimes difficult because committees often meet immediately prior to a board meeting.

A recommendation which has implications for departments which did not participate in its formation should be available for discussion before the recommendation is presented to the board for action. This may mean that the recommendation is given a first reading at the next meeting. This slows down the decision-making process, but when these steps are not taken, it is frequently necessary for a board to reconsider an action. This pacing is less objectionable when we recognize that we are dealing here with Ends issues and not administrative detail which needs immediate action.

The reporting should include a summary of the factors which led to the conclusion. When this is not done, boards often feel the need to redo the work of the committee.

EXHIBIT 6

Board's Appraisal
of the Chief Executive Officer

I. Background
  A. One necessary responsibility of a board is appraising the work of its CEO.
    1. Reasons why appraisal is needed:
      a. To improve the confidence, support, growth, and working relationship between the board and CEO.
      b. To assure the board, staff, and clients or customers that the mission, goals and plans, and program services or products of the organization are being achieved at the highest level possible or promised.
      c. To avoid painful, unnecessary separation of the CEO from the organization.
      d. To grant the CEO the satisfaction of a good appraisal.
    2. Some reasons why appraisals have been avoided, feared, skimped, or been done poorly:
      a. Fear of loss: "If we make her/him angry, she/he might quit." "Having her/him is better than having no one."
      b. Fear of someone getting upset.
      c. Fear of doing what seems tough.
      d. Fear of demands: "If we give her/him a good evaluation, s/he will demand more."
      e. Fear of the new: "We don't know how to evaluate well."
  B. Roles of the board and the CEO must be kept clear and must be followed to assure an effective organization. For example:
    1. The board focuses on mission, goals, values, policies, and managing the CEO.
    2. The CEO focuses on operations: planning, organizing, leading, assessing progress, managing personnel and finances, and achieving goals.

Exhibit 6

II. Process for evaluating the work of the CEO
    A. **Who** conducts the evaluation?
        The board chairperson, after full consultation with the board.
    B. **When?**
        A one- to two-hour session within a month after the annual report (fiscal and operations) of the CEO to the board.
    C. **Where?**
        In the CEO's or chairperson's office; not in a restaurant or informal setting.
    D. **How** is an evaluation conducted?
        1. Prepare a year in advance:
            a. Set goals for the CEO's performance (see Exhibit 7).
            b. Set standards to measure achievement of goals.
            c. Set procedures for assessing and discussing results.
        2. Begin with monthly (at least) supervision of the CEO by the chairperson. Agenda includes:
            a. Preparing the agenda for board meetings and reviewing board meetings.
            b. Reviewing the goals and standards of the organization and the procedures and progress toward those goals by the CEO.
            c. Morale of the organization.
            d. Relationships with other organizations.
            e. It is essential that both the chairperson and the CEO prepare for these sessions and that they keep careful records of these meetings.
        3. At year-end use an evaluation form which includes goals and standards of the CEO's performance (see Exhibit 7). It should be:
            a. Completed by the CEO to prepare for the appraisal.
            b. Completed by the board, separately, to prepare for the appraisal.
        4. The interview itself: The chairperson should propose the exact date for the interview soon after the annual report is completed by the CEO, although the time of the year for the evaluation should be set, known, and agreed upon a year in advance.

5. At the interview itself, the chairperson should lead the meeting, begin and close on time, and complete the process within a one- to two-hour time period.
6. The chairperson should conduct the interview by reviewing each item on the form, making sure both understand the appraisal and that a final appraisal is agreed upon.
7. The final conclusion to be communicated to the CEO is that the board has:
   a. Reaffirmed its positive feelings for the work of the CEO.
   b. Clarified any dissatisfaction they have with the CEO's work.
   c. Determined what changes of direction, priority, or effort for the coming year need to be made.
8. At the next monthly supervision session the CEO and chairperson should establish areas of accountability, standards, and procedures for the CEO's next year of work, as well as a method of evaluation.

E. On occasion, outside consultation might help a board in this evaluation process. If a board feels uncertain or fearful of the evaluation process, it is advisable to secure the help of a recommended consultant rather than not evaluating the work of the CEO.

F. The primary goal of the appraisal is to give support to the CEO, encouraging him/her in the tasks and loneliness of the role. Far less time should be given to expressing dissatisfaction unless major problems must be resolved.

EXHIBIT 7

A Performance Appraisal of the Chief Executive Officer

Check your appraisal of the CEO's work over the past fiscal year:

A = Outstanding
B = Expected
C = Below Expectation
D = Unacceptable

I. Planning

A   B   C   D

___ ___ ___ ___ A. The CEO works with the board to develop and implement a planning process that guides the organization into long-term and continued growth and that guides it toward achieving the larger mission of the organization.

___ ___ ___ ___ B. The CEO uses a long-range and annual planning process that involves the managers and supervisors in the organization (directly aimed at accomplishing the goals established by the board of directors).

___ ___ ___ ___ C. The CEO uses a budgeting process (with department participation) that involves annual and monthly targets for capital, income, and expense items.

___ ___ ___ ___ D. The CEO brings annual plans and budgets for accomplishing the goals of the organization to the board for approval on the agreed upon schedule.

___ ___ ___ ___ E. The CEO develops (so that the board can approve) policies and procedures that effectively help guide and designate actions of the staff toward the goals.

II. Organizing

A B C D

__ __ __ __ A. The CEO has developed and leads an organizational structure that is consistent with the organization's management philosophy and is effective in accomplishing its goals.

__ __ __ __ B. The CEO has developed and supports a development program for all employees that is preparing the organization for the future.

__ __ __ __ C. The organization has the most highly qualified, trained, and productive staff possible with a satisfactory turnover ratio.

III. Leading

A B C D

__ __ __ __ A. The CEO has an excellent communication system established in all areas of the organization, assuring adequate communication from anyone to anyone.

__ __ __ __ B. The CEO has a well developed performance appraisal system working in the organization which begins with an annual performance plan for each person.

__ __ __ __ C. The CEO understands how people are motivated toward work and is an effective leader in helping them to contribute their best to accomplishing the work of the organization. (This builds morale.)

Exhibit 7

IV. Controlling

A   B   C   D

___ ___ ___ ___   A. At the end of the year, income and expense budgets are within guidelines established at the beginning of the year.

___ ___ ___ ___   B. Effective supervisory processes are at work within the organization, resulting in:

1. Accomplishing goals;
2. Employees learning and growing;
3. Annual or more frequent performance appraisals;
4. Monthly or more frequent private communication with each employee by supervisor;
5. Strong teamwork.

V. Relationships

A   B   C   D

___ ___ ___ ___   A. The CEO has an effective relationship with community people, which assists the organization in accomplishing its goals.

___ ___ ___ ___   B. The CEO has an effective relationship with the board of directors, which assists the organization in accomplishing its goals.

___ ___ ___ ___   C. The CEO has an effective relationship with his/her immediate staff and all employees, which assists the organization in accomplishing its goals.

___ ___ ___ ___   D. The CEO has an effective relationship with customers and clients, which assists the organization in accomplishing its goals.

VI. Overall

A   B   C   D

___ ___ ___ ___   The CEO provides leadership for the organization's total activities that succeed in accomplishing the goals as established by the board of directors.

EXHIBIT 8

Annual Board Self-Assessment

Introduction

This procedure is intended first to help board members to be aware of their total task and, secondly, to insure that they are accomplishing that task. This approach may be altered to suit the circumstances of an individual organization, but some type of systematic evaluation procedure can help increase a board's effectiveness.

Suggested Procedure

1. The Board Self-Assessment is placed on the agenda of a future board meeting, and time is reserved accordingly. (This process does not need to be annual, but should be done every several years.)

2. The subject is introduced by the chair, who emphasizes its importance and explains what should be done with the evaluation forms. Provision should be made for absent directors to participate.

3. Board members may complete the forms while the meeting is in session and return them to the designated person—the chair, secretary, or chair of Board Services Committee—or take them home and return them in a few days.

4. The results are tabulated, summarized, reproduced, and distributed to the members.

5. Time is reserved at the next board meeting to discuss the issues that emerged from these assessments, placing them in order of priority and assigning them for appropriate follow-up.

Exhibit 8

Annual Board Self-Assessment

Instructions: Check "Yes," "No," or "Unc." (Uncertain).
Add ideas, questions, actions needed under "Notes."

ACTIVITIES	YES	NO	UNC.	NOTES
1. The board understands that its accountability includes financial responsibility, accounting and control, and social/ethical decisions.				
2. Good printed materials about the organization are available in an attractive and up-to-date format, and publicity appears in appropriate media in sufficient frequency and quality.				
3. The board represents the organization to the public, giving reports and listening to public needs and concerns.				
4. The board approves selection of outside counsel (attorney).				
RELATION TO CHIEF EXECUTIVE OFFICER				
5. The board selects a Chief Executive Officer and delegates to him/her full responsibility for all duties, except those reserved for the board.				
6. The board establishes an annual performance plan for the Chief Executive Officer and monitors and evaluates annually.				

	YES	NO	UNC.	NOTES
7. The board has a succession plan for the Chief Executive Officer and other designated key officers.				
APPROVES MISSION, POLICIES, GOALS, AND PLANS				
8. The mission, purposes, and values of the organization are clearly defined and approved by the board.				
9. The board approves an annual operations plan each year.				
10. General operating policies, personnel policies, and job descriptions are in writing, are easily accessible (in binder format), and are regularly updated.				
11. The organization meets all laws, regulations (local, state, national, international), and licensing or accreditation standards above and beyond the bare minimum required, including quality and safety.				
MONITORS FINANCIAL STRUCTURE AND ACTIVITY				
12. The board approves all changes in capital structure.				
13. The board approves an income and expense budget in line with policy.				

Exhibit 8

	YES	NO	UNC.	NOTES
14. The board approves and monitors all long- and short-term borrowing.				
15. Insurance coverage for board, staff, facilities, programs, etc. is monitored regularly.				
16. The board authorizes an annual independent financial audit and reviews the report with the auditor.				
17. The board authorizes all bank signatures.				
18. The board oversees all fund-raising activities.				
19. The board establishes financial procedures which are completely and accurately followed, including billing, accounts management, accounting, taxes, etc.				
MONITORS, REVIEWS, AND APPRAISES MANAGEMENT				
20. The board approves the operational/organizational relationships or changes departments, divisions, and lines of accountability as needed.				
21. The board reviews and approves compensation for key staff and a compensation plan for the total organization.				

	YES	NO	UNC.	NOTES
22. The board approves company benefit plans, pensions, profit sharing, stock plans, etc., or exceptions to plans as applicable.				
MONITORS PERFORMANCE OF MANAGEMENT				
23. The board receives and monitors—at least quarterly—financial, statistical, and operations reports.				
24. The board reviews and critiques staffs' deficiencies in performances and assists in remedies.				
RESPONSIBLE FOR MANAGEMENT OF THE BOARD				
25. The board operates with a clear and current set of bylaws with which all board members are familiar.				
26. Roles and responsibilities of board and committees are well defined and understood, with descriptions for each.				
27. The board provides for removal of board members for just cause; e.g., missing more than 20% of board meetings without excuse.				
28. New board members receive orientation in all aspects of the board's work.				

Exhibit 8

	YES	NO	UNC.	NOTES
29. The board creates committees of the board, defines their functions, and dissolves them as appropriate.				
30. The board has an executive committee to handle matters which may come up between meetings. Its authority is specified in the bylaws.				
31. Training for board work is a regular part of its annual plan.				
32. A procedure for appraisal of the board and individual member's performance is done regularly.				
BOARD MEETINGS				
33. All members actively participate in each meeting of the board and committees to which they are assigned.				
34. The board has an effective procedure for decision-making which it follows; all appropriate persons are involved in the process. Board meetings are effective.				
35. The board has executive sessions (without staff) regularly.				
36. The board has a regular report from the chair, as well as a report from the CEO.				

	YES	NO	UNC.	NOTES
37. Agenda and other board materials, including study documents, are mailed to members in sufficient time for review in advance of board meetings.				
38. Board and committee minutes are circulated to members soon after each meeting.				
39. There is a clear separation of board functions and responsibilities from management functions and responsibilities.				
40. Major proposals are thoroughly processed before they are presented and are available in written form.				

EXHIBIT 9

A More Excellent Way

We may speak the language of organizational structure and mission, but if we do not have love in our hearts for those who are intended to benefit from them, our efforts will have no more effect than a noisy gong or a clanging cymbal whose influence fades away with its clamor.

We may speak about Servant Leadership and clear lines of authority, we may have compelling strategies for organizational effectiveness and renewal, but if we have not love for people, it is all in vain. We may distribute our resources with the utmost efficiency and give our lives to save the world, but if love is not our motive, the world will be none the better for our effort.

With love we will be very patient and understanding as we interact with other cultures.

With love we will not feel boastfully righteous as though we have all the solutions to the world's needs.

With love we will never assert our superiority, never selfishly seek praise for sharing with others that with which we have been so abundantly blessed.

With love we will never inflate our ego at the expense of those we have come to serve.

With love we will always be slow to expose the failures and shortcomings of others.

With love we will not be resentful when our service is taken for granted.

Love never gives up. As for theories and strategies, they will be superseded; as for organizations, they will cease. For our planning and our institutions are incomplete, but when our actions are guided by love and justice, they will hit the mark.

We are limited in our understanding; we see in a mirror dimly. We are baffled by problems, and lasting solutions elude us. But we are learning bit by bit and we long for the day when love will rule the world.

Thus, faith that God has a plan for the world, hope that all can realize their human potential, and love that knows no boundaries—these three endure—but the greatest is love. Make love your goal.

—Edgar Stoesz, with gratitude to St. Paul (I Corinthians 13)
Adapted from *Beyond Good Intentions* by Edgar Stoesz

RECOMMENDED READINGS

Adizes, Ichak.
1988   *Corporate Life Cycles.* Englewood NJ: Prentice Hall.
  A detailed explanation of how organizations grow or do not grow, focusing on the needs of the organization itself.

Carver, John.
1990   *Boards That Make a Difference.* San Francisco: Jossey-Bass.
  This is a sophisticated, doctrinaire book that is quite useful to mature boards or boards that want to lead their organiztion and themselves to maturity.

DePree, Max.
1989   *The Art of Leadership.* New York: Dell Publishing.
  An inspirational description of participative management in a very successful for-profit business that nonprofits should learn from.

Drucker, Peter F.
1990   *Nonprofit Management and Leadership, Vol. 1.* San Francisco: Jossey & Bass.

Eadie, Douglas C.
  Beyond Strategic Planning. National Center for Nonprofit Boards, 2000 L Street NW, Suite 411, Washington DC, 20036.

Fisher, Roger and William Ury.
1981   *Getting to Yes.* Boston: Houghton-Mifflin Co.
  Practical steps to negotiating everything from everyday family decisions to corporate strategies.

Greenleaf, Robert.
1977   *Servant Leadership.* New York: Paulist Press.
  Practical implications and methods for "If any one among you would be chief, let him be the servant of all."

Kotter, John P.
1990   *A Force for Change.* New York: The Free Press.
  A useful description of the difference and need for leadership as compared to management.

Recommended Readings

Lai, Mary L.
Am I Covered? Consortium for Human Services, Box 1183, San Jose, CA, 95108.

Leas, Speed B.
Moving Your Church Through Conflict. Alban Institute, 4125 Nebraska NW, Washington DC, 20016.

Mueller, Robert K.
Smarter Board Meetings: For Effective Board Governance. National Center for Nonprofit Boards, 2000 L Street NW, Suite 411, Washington DC, 20036.

Meuller, Robert K.
Understanding Nonprofit Financial Statements: A Primer for Board Members. National Center for Nonprofit Boards, 2000 L Street NW, Suite 411, Washington DC, 20036.

O'Connell, Brian.
1985   *The Board Member Book.* Washington DC: The Foundation Center.

Park, Dabrey.
Strategic Planning and the Nonprofit Board. National Center for Nonprofit Boards, 2000 L Street NW, Suite 411, Washington DC, 20036.

Salamon, Lester M.
1992   *America's Nonprofit Sector: A Primer.* Baltimore, MD: Johns Hopkins University Press.

Senge, Peter M.
1990   *The Fifth Discipline.* New York: Doubleday.
A detailed projection for helping organizations to be "learning" organizations.

"Papers on Conciliation." Mennonite Central Committee, 21 South 12th Street, Akron, PA, 17501.

Strategic Planning for Nonprofits. Support Center of America, 2001 O Street NW, Washington DC, 20036-5955.

INDEX

Index

ABOUT THE AUTHORS

Edgar Stoesz has spent most of his adult life in a nonprofit setting, both as director and employee. A native Minnesotan, he held six different administrative posts with the Mennonite Central Committee, including seven years as Associate Executive Secretary, retiring in 1987. Simultaneously he served as President and CEO of Mennonite Indemnity, with plans to retire during 1994.

Since 1990 he has served as chair of Habitat for Humanity, International, having held the same position with Heifer Project, International from 1979-1982. From 1974-1985 he served on the Executive Committee of Mennonite Economic Development Associates. Currently he is active on the boards of the Grant Foundation, the American Leprosy Mission, International, and the Mutual Aid Societies.

His administrative responsibilities have taken him to more than 50 countries. He has contributed articles to church papers and addressed audiences on subjects related to his service. He wrote the book, *Beyond Good Intentions* (1972), while on sabbatical leave at Cornell University.

Chester A. Raber, Ph.D., is a longtime organization and management consultant working with both for-profit and not-for-profit organizations. He has focused on organization assessment and development, with particular attention to team-building, and management development, with particular attention to executive development.

He recently retired from Greenfield Associates, a private consulting firm which he founded and led from 1981-1992. Greenfield Associates was a subsidiary of High Industries, Inc., Lancaster, Pennsylvania.

He has worked with many nonprofit boards, helping to establish, guide, and plan with them. His client list of boards includes hospitals, mental health organizations, retirement communities, organizations, colleges, communications enterprises, police, and others. He has paid special attention to the relationship between the chief executive officer and chairperson.

In other circumstances he has been chairman, officer, and member of numerous nonprofit boards.

Doing Good Better!
Order Form

If you would like to order copies of **Doing Good Better!** for boards you know or are part of, use this form. (Discounts apply for more than one copy.) Photocopy this page as often as you like.

The following discounts apply:

1 copy	$9.95
2-5 copies	$8.96 each (a 10% discount)
6-10 copies	$8.46 each (a 15% discount)
11-20 copies	$7.96 each (a 20% discount)

Prices subject to change.

Quantity   *Price*   *Total*

_____ copies of **Doing Good Better!** @ _____   _____

PA residents add 6% sales tax _____

Shipping & Handling
(add 10%, $2.50 minimum) _____

TOTAL _____

(Please fill in the payment and shipping information on the other side.)

METHOD OF PAYMENT

❒   Check or Money Order
    (payable to Good Books in U.S. funds)

❒   Please charge my:
    ❒   MasterCard   ❒   Visa

#_____

exp. date _____

Signature _____

Name_____

Address _____

City _____

State_____

Zip _____

SHIP TO: *(if different)*

Name_____

Address _____

City _____

State_____

Zip _____

Mail order to **Good Books**
P.O. Box 419
Intercourse, PA 17534-0419
Call toll-free 800/762-7171
In Canada call collect 717/768-7171
Fax number 717/768-3433

Prices subject to change.